TABLE OF CONTENTS

Date: 12/18/18

**372.1262 FLO
Florida state assessments,
grade 4 mathematics success**

Success Strategies

This section contains a list of test-taking strategies that you may find helpful as you work through the test. By taking what you know and applying logical thought, you can maximize your chances of answering any question correctly!

It is very important to realize that every question is different and every person is different: no single strategy will work on every question, and no single strategy will work for every person. That's why we've included all of them here, so you can try them out and determine which ones work best for different types of questions and which ones work best for you.

Question Strategies

Read Carefully

Read the question and answer choices carefully. Don't miss the question because you misread the terms. You have plenty of time to read each question thoroughly and make sure you understand what is being asked. Yet a happy medium must be attained, so don't waste too much time. You must read carefully, but efficiently.

Contextual Clues

Look for contextual clues. If the question includes a word you are not familiar with, look at the immediate context for some indication of what the word might mean. Contextual clues can often give you all the information you need to decipher the meaning of an unfamiliar word. Even if you can't determine the meaning, you may be able to narrow down the possibilities enough to make a solid guess at the answer to the question.

Prefixes

If you're having trouble with a word in the question or answer choices, try dissecting it. Take advantage of every clue that the word might include. Prefixes and suffixes can be a huge help. Usually they allow you to determine a basic meaning. Pre- means before, post- means after, pro - is positive, de- is negative. From prefixes and suffixes, you can get an idea of the general meaning of the word and try to put it into context.

Hedge Words

Watch out for critical hedge words, such as *likely, may, can, sometimes, often, almost, mostly, usually, generally, rarely,* and *sometimes.* Question writers insert these hedge phrases to cover every possibility. Often an answer choice will be wrong simply because it leaves no room for exception. Be on guard for answer choices that have definitive words such as *exactly* and *always.*

Switchback Words

Stay alert for *switchbacks.* These are the words and phrases frequently used to alert you to shifts in thought. The most common switchback words are *but, although,* and *however.* Others include *nevertheless, on the other hand, even though, while, in spite of, despite, regardless of.* Switchback words are important to catch because they can change the direction of the question or an answer choice.

Face Value

When in doubt, use common sense. Accept the situation in the problem at face value. Don't read too much into it. These problems will not require you to make wild assumptions. If you have to go beyond creativity and warp time or space in order to have an answer choice fit the question, then you should move on and consider the other answer choices. These are normal problems rooted in reality. The applicable relationship or explanation may not be readily apparent, but it is there for you to figure out. Use your common sense to interpret anything that isn't clear.

Answer Choice Strategies

Answer Selection

The most thorough way to pick an answer choice is to identify and eliminate wrong answers until only one is left, then confirm it is the correct answer. Sometimes an answer choice may immediately seem right, but be careful. The test writers will usually put more than one reasonable answer choice on each question, so take a second to read all of them and make sure that the other choices are not equally obvious. As long as you have time left, it is better to read every answer choice than to pick the first one that looks right without checking the others.

Answer Choice Families

An answer choice family consists of two (in rare cases, three) answer choices that are very similar in construction and cannot all be true at the same time. If you see two answer choices that are direct opposites or parallels, one of them is usually the correct answer. For instance, if one answer choice says that quantity x increases and another either says that quantity x decreases (opposite) or says that quantity y increases (parallel), then those answer choices would fall into the same family. An answer choice that doesn't match the construction of the answer choice family is more likely to be incorrect. Most questions will not have answer choice families, but when they do appear, you should be prepared to recognize them.

Eliminate Answers

Eliminate answer choices as soon as you realize they are wrong, but make sure you consider all possibilities. If you are eliminating answer choices and realize that the last one you are left with is also wrong, don't panic. Start over and consider each choice again. There may be something you missed the first time that you will realize on the second pass.

Avoid Fact Traps

Don't be distracted by an answer choice that is factually true but doesn't answer the question. You are looking for the choice that answers the question. Stay focused on what the question is asking for so you don't accidentally pick an answer that is true but incorrect. Always go back to the question and make sure the answer choice you've selected actually answers the question and is not merely a true statement.

Extreme Statements

In general, you should avoid answers that put forth extreme actions as standard practice or proclaim controversial ideas as established fact. An answer choice that states the "process should be used in certain situations, if..." is much more likely to be correct than one that states the "process should be discontinued completely." The first is a calm rational statement and doesn't even make a definitive, uncompromising stance, using a hedge word *if* to provide wiggle room, whereas the second choice is a radical idea and far more extreme.

Benchmark

As you read through the answer choices and you come across one that seems to answer the question well, mentally select that answer choice. This is not your final answer, but it's the one that will help you evaluate the other answer choices. The one that you selected is your benchmark or standard for judging each of the other answer choices. Every other answer choice must be compared to your benchmark. That choice is correct until proven otherwise by another answer choice beating it. If you find a better answer, then that one becomes your new benchmark. Once you've decided that no other choice answers the question as well as your benchmark, you have your final answer.

Predict the Answer

Before you even start looking at the answer choices, it is often best to try to predict the answer. When you come up with the answer on your own, it is easier to avoid distractions and traps because you will know exactly what to look for. The right answer choice is unlikely to be word-for-word what you came up with, but it should be a close match. Even if you are confident that you have the right answer, you should still take the time to read each option before moving on.

General Strategies

Tough Questions

If you are stumped on a problem or it appears too hard or too difficult, don't waste time. Move on! Remember though, if you can quickly check for obviously incorrect answer choices, your chances of guessing correctly are greatly improved. Before you completely give up, at least try to knock out a couple of possible answers. Eliminate what you can and then guess at the remaining answer choices before moving on.

Check Your Work

Since you will probably not know every term listed and the answer to every question, it is important that you get credit for the ones that you do know. Don't miss any questions through careless mistakes. If at all possible, try to take a second to look back over your answer selection and make sure you've selected the correct answer choice and haven't made a costly careless mistake (such as marking an answer choice that you didn't mean to mark). This quick double check should more than pay for itself in caught mistakes for the time it costs.

Pace Yourself

It's easy to be overwhelmed when you're looking at a page full of questions; your mind is confused and full of random thoughts, and the clock is ticking down faster than you would like. Calm down and maintain the pace that you have set for yourself. Especially as you get down to the last few minutes of the test, don't let the small numbers on the clock make you panic. As long as you are on track by monitoring your pace, you are guaranteed to have time for each question.

Don't Rush

It is very easy to make errors when you are in a hurry. Maintaining a fast pace in answering questions is pointless if it makes you miss questions that you would have gotten right otherwise. Test writers like to include distracting information and wrong answers that seem right. Taking a little extra time to avoid careless mistakes can make all the difference in your test score. Find a pace that allows you to be confident in the answers that you select.

Keep Moving

Panicking will not help you pass the test, so do your best to stay calm and keep moving. Taking deep breaths and going through the answer elimination steps you practiced can help to break through a stress barrier and keep your pace.

Final Notes

The combination of a solid foundation of content knowledge and the confidence that comes from practicing your plan for applying that knowledge is the key to maximizing your performance on test day. As your foundation of content knowledge is built up and strengthened, you'll find that the strategies included in this chapter become more and more effective in helping you quickly sift through the distractions and traps of the test to isolate the correct answer.

Now it's time to move on to the test content chapters of this book, but be sure to keep your goal in mind. As you read, think about how you will be able to apply this information on the test. If you've already seen sample questions for the test and you have an idea of the question format and style, try to come up with questions of your own that you can answer based on what you're reading. This will give you valuable practice applying your knowledge in the same ways you can expect to on test day.

Good luck and good studying!

Lesson 1

Place Value 1-100,000

 The place value of a digit is determined by where it is in a number.

Hundred Thousands	Ten Thousands	Thousands	Hundreds	Tens	Ones
1	2	3	4	5	6

1 2 3, 4 5 6

One Hundred Twenty Three Thousand, Four Hundred Fifty Six

Write these numbers correctly in the blanks.

1. 422,719 =

4	2	2	7	1	9
Hundred Thousands	Ten Thousands	Thousands	Hundreds	Tens	Ones

2. 982,124 =

Hundred Thousands	Ten Thousands	Thousands	Hundreds	Tens	Ones

3. 263,927 =

Hundred Thousands	Ten Thousands	Thousands	Hundreds	Tens	Ones

4. 627,141 =

Hundred Thousands	Ten Thousands	Thousands	Hundreds	Tens	Ones

5. 891,362 =

Hundred Thousands	Ten Thousands	Thousands	Hundreds	Tens	Ones

Place Value Big numbers 1-1,000,000

The place value of a digit is determined by where it is in a number.

Millions	Hundred Thousands	Ten Thousands	Thousands	Hundreds	Tens	Ones
1	2	3	4	5	6	7

1,234,567

One million, two hundred thirty-four thousand, five hundred sixty-seven

1. 6,138,462 =

6	1	3	8	4	6	2
Millions	Hundred Thousands	Ten Thousands	Thousands	Hundreds	Tens	Ones

2. 3,194,675 =

Millions	Hundred Thousands	Ten Thousands	Thousands	Hundreds	Tens	Ones

3. 8,417,205 =

Millions	Hundred Thousands	Ten Thousands	Thousands	Hundreds	Tens	Ones

4. 2,765,447 =

Millions	Hundred Thousands	Ten Thousands	Thousands	Hundreds	Tens	Ones

5. 5,925,057 =

Millions	Hundred Thousands	Ten Thousands	Thousands	Hundreds	Tens	Ones

Lesson 2

Identifying Place Value - Word Problems

Solve the word problems below.

1. In the number 25,483 :
   A. This digit is in the ones place _____
   B. This digit is in the hundreds place _____
   C. The 5 is in the _____ place
   D. The 8 is in the _____ place

2. In the number 62,134 :
   A. This digit is in the tens place _____
   B. This digit is in the thousands place _____
   C. The 6 is in the _____ place
   D. The 4 is in the _____ place

3. In the number 84,327 :
   A. This digit is in the ones place _____
   B. This digit is in the thousands place _____
   C. The 2 is in the _____ place
   D. The 8 is in the _____ place

4. In the number 14,960 :
   A. This digit is in the hundreds place _____
   B. This digit is in the ten-thousands place _____
   C. The 0 is in the _____ place
   D. The 4 is in the _____ place

5. In the number 40,589 :
   A. This digit is in the ones place _____
   B. This digit is in the hundreds place _____
   C. The 0 is in the _____ place
   D. The 4 is in the _____ place

Lesson 3

Rounding up to 10,000

Round the following numbers to the nearest hundred.

1. 891 ___900___
2. 212 _____
3. 602 _____
4. 598 _____
5. 775 _____
6. 349 _____
7. 239 _____
8. 621 _____
9. 440 _____
10. 112 _____

Round the following numbers to the nearest thousand.

11. 9,054 _____
12. 3,567 _____
13. 2,969 _____
14. 6,056 _____
15. 7,476 _____
16. 2,113 _____
17. 8,631 _____
18. 5,589 _____
19. 1,551 _____
20. 4,999 _____

Round the following numbers to the nearest ten-thousand.

21. 49,508 _____
22. 72,497 _____
23. 12,023 _____
24. 51,515 _____
25. 88,720 _____
26. 42,023 _____
27. 20,653 _____
28. 13,749 _____

Rounding up to 100,000

Round the following numbers to the nearest thousand.

1.	2,563 _____	**6.**	4,219 _____
2.	9,198 _____	**7.**	5,756 _____
3.	1,423 _____	**8.**	8,154 _____
4.	7,712 _____	**9.**	6,069 _____
5.	3,300 _____	**10**	1,995 _____

Round the following numbers to the nearest ten-thousand.

11.	39,092 _____	**16.**	77,150 _____
12.	19,917 _____	**17.**	33,809 _____
13.	93,254 _____	**18.**	35,451 _____
14.	56,055 _____	**19.**	20,901 _____
15.	70,856 _____	**20.**	48,599 _____

Round the following numbers to the nearest hundred-thousand.

21.	274,333 _____	**26.**	317,110 _____
22.	596,559 _____	**27.**	882,658 _____
23.	221,324 _____	**28.**	610,567 _____
24.	530,708 _____	**29.**	789,381 _____
25.	189,365 _____	**30.**	109,277 _____

Lesson 4

Expanded Form

We learned earlier that every digit in a number has a place value. **Expanded form** shows that number expanded into an addition statement.

Example:

The expanded form of 5,786 is:
5,000 + 700 + 80 + 6.

Write each number in expanded form.

1. 82   **2.** 29   **3.** 56   **4.** 74

80 + 2   _____   _____   _____

5. 35   **6.** 99   **7.** 250   **8.** 629

_____   _____   _____   _____

9. 150   **10.** 892   **11.** 905   **12.** 427

_____   _____   _____   _____

13. Twenty - Nine   **14.** Seventy - One   **15.** Eighty - Six

20 + 9   _____   _____

16. Fifty - Four   **17.** Sixteen   **18.** Thirty - Eight

_____   _____   _____

Expanded Form 2

Write each number in expanded form.

1.   156   **2.**   658   **3.**   295   **4.**   431

_____   _____   _____   _____

5.   567   **6.**   155   **7.**   832   **8.**   394

_____   _____   _____   _____

9.   2,591   **10.**   8,942   **11.**   4,154

_____   _____   _____

12.   6,387   **13.**   1,582   **14.**   3,578

_____   _____   _____

15.   44,658   **16.**   73,435

_____   _____

17.   95,261   **18.**   37,872

_____   _____

Lesson 5

Ordering up to 10,000

Write these numbers in order from least to greatest.

1. 9,289 | 92,891 | 9,281 | 96,381   9,281   9,289   92,891   96,381

2. 23,112 | 23,111 | 22,311 | 2,313 _____

3. 7,856 | 7,855 | 78,855 | 78,856 _____

4. 11,112 | 1,111 | 11,131 | 10,112 _____

5. 4,326 | 44,326 | 44,436 | 4,316 _____

6. 3,289 | 3,891 | 3,819 | 3,818 _____

7. 57,289 | 57,891 | 57,211 | 57,500 _____

8. 60,255 | 6,552 | 66,252 | 6,255 _____

9. 15,247 | 15,250 | 15,248 | 15,249 _____

10. 9,564 | 92,564 | 9,546 | 93,564 _____

11. 8,219 | 84,921 | 84,218 | 84,219 _____

Ordering up to 100,000

Write these numbers in order from least to greatest.

1. 100,289 | 100,891 | 100,280 | 100,381 _____

2. 512,112 | 512,123 | 51,110 | 512,101 _____

3. 855,622 | 865,622 | 856,628 | 856,629 _____

4. 634,209 | 634,101 | 635,700 | 633,601 _____

5. 231,115 | 20,115 | 231,150 | 21,115 _____

6. 546,029 | 546,209 | 546,030 | 546,020 _____

7. 375,787 | 355,891 | 355,111 | 375,375 _____

8. 23,151 | 239,151 | 237,151 | 240,151 _____

9. 155,289 | 146,891 | 145,280 | 145,381 _____

10. 269,722 | 20,722 | 269,772 | 266,722 _____

11. 990,281 | 90,821 | 90,280 | 90,281 _____

12. 175,337 | 76,337 | 75,337 | 7,537 _____

Lesson 6

Number Patterns to 10,000

Complete the number patterns.

1. 10,475 | 10,485 | __10,495__ | __11,005__

2. 98,211 | _____ | _____ | 98,511

3. _____ | 62,001 | _____ | 64,001

4. 22,729 | 22,829 | _____ | _____

5. _____ | 82,657 | _____ | 84,657

6. 2,475 | 2,485 | _____ | _____

7. 11,303 | _____ | _____ | 14,303

8. _____ | 42,370 | _____ | 44,370

9. 72,112 | 72,119 | _____ | _____

10. 33,776 | _____ | _____ | 36,776

12. _____ | 79,061 | _____ | 99,061

Number Patterns to 100,000

Complete the number patterns.

1. 980,211 | _____ | _____ | 980,511

2. _____ | 621,001 | _____ | 619,001

3. 282,729 | 282,829 | _____ | _____

4. _____ | 694,657 | _____ | 694,677

5. 111,729 | 112,729 | _____ | _____

6. _____ | 350,001 | _____ | 352,001

7. 523,303 | _____ | _____ | 526,303

8. _____ | 815,370 | _____ | 825,370

9. _____ | 256,119 | 356,119 | _____

10. 609,776 | _____ | _____ | 639,776

11. 110,383 | 115,383 | _____ | _____

12. 340,303 | _____ | _____ | 370,303

Lesson 1

2-Digit Addition - Regrouping 1

To add multiple digit numbers together, start in the ones place and then use basic addition rules. When the number equals ten or more the first digit carries over to the next spot. This is called **regrouping**.

	Hundreds	Tens	Ones
Step 1: Add the digits in the ones column.		8	5
	+	1	7
			[2]

	Hundreds	Tens	Ones
Step 2: Carry the 1 over to the top of the tens column.		1	
		8	5
x		1	7
		①	2

	Hundreds	Tens	Ones
Step 3: Add all the digits in the tens column together.		1	
		8	5
x	+ 1	7
	[1] [0]	2

Solve the problems below.

1. 49
    + 3 2
    ———
    8 1

2. 5 8
    +   7
    ———

3. 8 3
    + 8 4
    ———

4. 4 2
    +   9
    ———

5. 5 2
    + 7 2
    ———

6. 4 4
    +   5
    ———

7. 3 2
    + 1 4
    ———

8. 1 8
    + 2 0
    ———

9. 7 1
    + 9 2
    ———

10. 5 9
    +   6
    ———

11. 8 1
    +   9
    ———

12. 6 0
    + 5 7
    ———

13. 3 2
    + 4 0
    ———

14. 1 9
    +   2
    ———

15. 2 7
    + 8 6
    ———

Lesson 2

2-Digit Addition - Regrouping 2

 To add multiple digit numbers together, start in the ones place and then use basic addition rules. When the number equals ten or more the first digit carries over to the next spot. This is called **regrouping**.

Solve the problems below.

1. 78
  +14

2. 64
  +39

3. 79
  +99

4. 34
  +75

5. 49
  +29

6. 58
  +87

7. 15
  +46

8. 27
  +67

9. 70
  +49

10. 13
  + 9

11. 35
  +68

12. 80
  +27

13. 48
  +24

14. 34
  +57

15. 55
  +37

16. 99
  +56

17. 68
  +68

18. 40
  +85

19. 74
  +66

20. 63
  +99

Lesson 3

2-Digit 3-Row Addition - Regrouping 1

To add multiple digit numbers together, start in the ones place and then use basic addition rules. When the number equals ten or more the first digit carries over to the next spot. This is called **regrouping**.

Solve the problems below.

1. 36
    22
  + 15
  ___

2. 84
    70
  + 9
  ___

3. 64
    29
  + 42
  ___

4. 57
    52
  + 73
  ___

5. 44
    15
  + 39
  ___

6. 66
    99
  + 82
  ___

7. 50
    36
  + 55
  ___

8. 15
    35
  + 80
  ___

9. 67
    72
  + 18
  ___

10. 11
     28
   + 37
   ___

11. 62
     97
   + 19
   ___

12. 55
     20
   + 12
   ___

13. 18
     19
   + 20
   ___

14. 22
     76
   + 8
   ___

15. 77
     37
   + 47
   ___

16. 46
     44
   + 56
   ___

17. 98
     49
   + 89
   ___

18. 75
     57
   + 6
   ___

19. 36
     62
   + 19
   ___

20. 99
     95
   + 92
   ___

2-Digit 3-Row Addition - Regrouping 2

To add multiple digit numbers together, start in the ones place
and then use basic addition rules. When the number equals
ten or more the first digit carries over to the next spot.
This is called **regrouping**.

Solve the problems below.

1. 12 60 + 42	**2.** 72 44 + 55	**3.** 72 16 + 11	**4.** 30 82 + 8	**5.** 23 67 + 94
6. 50 32 + 86	**7.** 24 72 + 39	**8.** 81 12 + 4	**9.** 96 64 + 51	**10.** 75 11 + 70
11. 44 79 + 93	**12.** 88 52 + 6	**13.** 20 36 + 24	**14.** 99 85 + 13	**15.** 60 92 + 41
16. 30 57 + 94	**17.** 77 12 + 9	**18.** 10 28 + 96	**19.** 92 68 + 47	**20.** 17 29 + 3

Lesson 4

Addition Word Problems

Use addition to solve the problems below.

1. Elle picked apples for four days. On day one she picked 10 apples. On day two she picked 26 apples. On day three she picked 14 apples. On day four she picked 14 apples. How many apples does Elle have in total?

_____

2. Cindy has been doing her chores every day after school. On Monday she swept the floor for 12 minutes. On Tuesday she spent 9 minutes making her bed. On Wednesday she washed the dishes for 20 minutes. On Thursday she spent 15 minutes vacuuming the floor. How much time did she spend on her chores?

_____

3. Steven is good at basketball. In game one he scored 14 points. In game two he scored 22 points. In game three he scored 27. In games four and five he scored 17 and 12 points. How many points has Steven scored so far?

_____

4. Amy loves to read. She reads every day after school. One day she read 45 minutes. The next day she read 30 minutes. The day after that she spent 57 minutes reading. Yesterday she read for 26 minutes and today she spent 15 minutes reading her book. How much time has she spent reading this week?

_____

Lesson 5

3-Digit Addition - Regrouping 1

To add multiple-digit numbers together, start in the ones place and then use basic addition rules. When a number equals ten or more the first digit carries over to the next spot. This is called **regrouping**.

Step 1: Add the digits in the one's column and carry over the 1 to the ten's column.	**Step 2:** Next add the digits in the tens's column and carry over the 1 to the hundred's column.	**Step 3:** Next add the digits in the hundred's column.	**Step 4:** Finally, carry over the 1 from the hundred's column to the thousands's column.

1000's	100's	10's	1's
		1	
	6	4	3
+	5	8	9
			2

1000's	100's	10's	1's
	1	1	
	6	4	3
+	5	8	9
		3	2

1000's	100's	10's	1's
	1	1	
	6	4	3
+	5	8	9
	2	3	2

1000's	100's	10's	1's
	1	1	
	6	4	3
+	5	8	9
1	2	3	2

Solve the problems below. Use regrouping when needed.

1. 498
   +321
   ─────
    819

2. 580
   +729

3. 134
   + 22

4. 309
   +447

5. 253
   +203

6. 171
   + 82

7. 344
   +493

8. 714
   +507

9. 629
   + 78

10. 629
   +351

3-Digit Addition - Regrouping 2

Solve the problems below using regrouping.

1. 151
    +459

2. 239
    +205

3. 677
    +380

4. 406
    +312

5. 951
    +123

6. 705
    +357

7. 824
    +199

8. 901
    +699

9. 333
    +178

10. 101
     +752

11. 509
     +456

12. 712
     + 55

13. 278
     +333

14. 158
     +207

15. 199
     +682

16. 999
     +715

17. 508
     +349

18. 724
     +924

19. 911
     +667

20. 507
     +133

Lesson 6

3-Digit 3-Row Addition - Regrouping

To add multiple digit numbers together, start in the ones place and then use basic addition rules. When the number equals ten or more the first digit carries over to the next spot. This is called **regrouping**.

Solve the problems below using regrouping.

1. 209	**2.** 456	**3.** 652	**4.** 572	**5.** 711
158	41	189	267	209
+ 472	+ 137	+ 305	+ 453	+ 374
839				

6. 455	**7.** 501	**8.** 782	**9.** 955	**10.** 389
126	472	106	572	411
+ 907	+ 904	+ 313	+ 117	+ 354

11. 111	**12.** 254	**13.** 715	**14.** 742	**15.** 958
684	906	355	279	144
+ 243	+ 145	+ 742	+ 109	+ 302

16. 621	**17.** 322	**18.** 752	**19.** 884	**20.** 308
435	532	962	222	144
+ 905	+ 814	+ 103	+ 606	+ 722

3-Digit 3-Row Addition - Regrouping 2

To add multiple digit numbers together, start in the ones place and then use basic addition rules. When the number equals ten or more the first digit carries over to the next spot. This is called **regrouping**.

Solve the problems below using regrouping.

1.   643
    207
+318
	2. 119
	  875
	+ 40
		3. 307
		  458
		+156
			4. 678
			  152
			+306
				5. 819
				  644
				+278

6.   339
  107
+389
	7. 712
	  263
	+140
		8. 181
		  396
		+ 15
			9. 899
			  295
			+590
				10. 165
				  980
				+263

11. 752
  310
+726
	12. 157
	  682
	+898
		13. 208
		  489
		+912
			14. 257
			  367
			+ 6
				15. 700
				  973
				+275

16. 661
  894
+ 64
	17. 313
	  578
	+149
		18. 985
		  405
		+123
			19. 785
			  246
			+385
				20. 222
				  746
				+118

Lesson 7

4-Digit Addition - Regrouping

Solve the problems below using regrouping.

1. 6895
  + 5406
  ———
  12301

2. 1259
  + 9502
  ———

3. 9543
  + 7845
  ———

4. 4051
  + 1150
  ———

5. 8507
  + 9847
  ———

6. 3250
  + 406
  ———

7. 2470
  + 3357
  ———

8. 1589
  + 6875
  ———

9. 5579
  + 6077
  ———

10. 1089
  + 2786
  ———

11. 7750
  + 597
  ———

12. 3378
  + 4508
  ———

13. 6917
  + 7502
  ———

14. 4329
  + 999
  ———

15. 9948
  + 113
  ———

16. 4705
  + 4866
  ———

17. 1580
  + 3987
  ———

18. 2778
  + 4891
  ———

19. 5576
  + 569
  ———

20. 3520
  + 1339
  ———

Lesson 8

4-Digit 3-Row Addition - Regrouping

Solve the problems below using regrouping.

1. 1091
     2157
    +3267
    ―――――
     6515

2. 9815
     4803
    +2216
    ―――――

3. 3891
     1259
    +7520
    ―――――

4. 2552
     8406
    +2271
    ―――――

5. 5330
     1211
    +9801
    ―――――

6. 4881
     2009
    +1987
    ―――――

7. 3072
     1650
    +1578
    ―――――

8. 1985
     8105
    +1776
    ―――――

9. 9841
     2750
    +1349
    ―――――

10. 5400
      7501
     +3814
     ―――――

11. 7072
      6152
     +1785
     ―――――

12. 1707
      1804
     +2950
     ―――――

13. 2400
      3962
     +8815
     ―――――

14. 6074
      1255
     +8079
     ―――――

15. 8180
      2755
     +2577
     ―――――

16. 9064
      9607
     +6074
     ―――――

17. 4911
      2757
     +3025
     ―――――

18. 5787
      6962
     +1570
     ―――――

19. 7705
      5321
     +1766
     ―――――

20. 3033
      1447
     +9632
     ―――――

Lesson 9

5-Digit Addition - Regrouping

Solve the problems below using regrouping.

1. 1 5,8 0 1 + 3 5,8 4 7 ———— 5 1 6 4 8	**2.** 7 5,2 1 1 + 2 5,7 8 6	**3.** 8 9,0 5 7 + 1 1,0 5 9	**4.** 3 3,5 2 0 + 6,5 7 9
5. 4 0,5 1 7 + 1 2,5 2 3	**6.** 7 4,2 5 9 + 6 9,8 0 5	**7.** 9 4,5 2 1 + 7,0 8 9	**8.** 3 0,6 7 1 + 3 1,3 3 7
9. 4 5,9 9 4 + 2 7,8 8 1	**10.** 6 5,8 1 7 + 5,8 4 7	**11.** 1 1,0 7 2 + 3 6,6 9 8	**12.** 3 2,5 0 1 + 4,8 7 9
13. 9 0,1 1 7 + 1 5,2 5 7	**14.** 8 5,0 2 4 + 9 6,3 1 2	**15.** 5 7,7 8 1 + 5,6 9 0	**16.** 7 8,5 2 1 + 3 6,9 0 1
17. 5 8,5 2 0 + 5 7,9 3 6	**18.** 3 0,2 5 8 + 2 8,5 2 7	**19.** 7 8,2 6 9 + 1 0,2 5 4	**20.** 6 3,3 9 1 + 6 0,5 8 2

- 34 -

Lesson 10

5-Digit Addition – Regrouping 2

Solve the problems below using regrouping.

1. 6 8,5 0 2
    + 3 5,8 4 7

2. 3 2,0 0 0
    + 1 7,8 1 5

3. 4 9,2 1 5
    + 2 1,5 8 9

4. 6 5,1 0 7
    + 4 2,2 3 8

5. 8 6,0 1 1
    + 3 2,9 9 7

6. 9 1,0 5 8
    + 1 5,2 1 1

7. 7 0,1 2 2
    + 6 2,9 3 9

8. 2 9,0 0 6
    + 1 1,2 7 1

9. 5 5,1 2 7
    + 1 7,5 6 8

10. 2 5,0 8 7
    + 9,1 7 5

11. 4 9,1 8 6
    + 2 3,2 5 0

12. 9 5,1 1 8
    + 3,9 3 5

13. 7 7,1 1 7
    + 5 9,9 9 0

14. 4 5,7 1 0
    + 3 6,3 0 3

15. 6 7,1 8 1
    + 2,6 2 8

16. 8 2,2 0 7
    + 6 0,8 4 5

17. 4 5,3 8 7
    + 3 6,1 0 5

18. 7 7,0 0 7
    + 1 1,3 6 7

19. 6 0,1 1 7
    + 4 6,2 8 9

20. 8 4,9 9 9
    + 2 6,1 1 1

Lesson 1

2-Digit Subtraction - Borrowing 1

To subtract and borrow , start with the ones column. If the bottom number is of a greater value, you have to borrow from the next column.

Step 1: If the bottom number is a greater value than the top number, you need to borrow.	Tens | Ones 8 | 4 - 1 | 9	**Step 2:** Borrow 10 from the next column. Reducing the 8 to 7 and increasing 4 to 14. Now we are ready to subtract.	Tens | Ones 7 8̸ | ¹4 - 1 | 9 | 5	**Step 3:** Finish by subtracting the numbers in the tens column.	Tens | Ones 7 8̸ | ¹4 - 1 | 9 6 | 5

Use borrowing to solve the problems below.

1. 3 5	2. 5 4	3. 8 3	4. 4 2	5. 5 6
− 6	− 2 8	− 4	− 1 5	− 9
2 9				

6. 4 1	7. 8 2	8. 1 6	9. 7 1	10. 5 2
− 5	− 5 9	− 7	− 3	− 2 8

11. 8 7	12. 3 4	13. 7 2	14. 2 1	15. 9 1
− 5 9	− 6	− 3 5	− 2	− 4 4

2-Digit Subtraction - Borrowing 2

Use borrowing to solve the problems below.

1. 44	2. 64	3. 37	4. 66	5. 55
- 3 5	- 5	- 1 9	- 7	- 1 7

6. 50	7. 88	8. 25	9. 72	10. 32
- 2 7	- 3 6	- 1 6	- 5 3	- 2 9

11. 44	12. 90	13. 29	14. 65	15. 78
- 1 7	- 7 6	- 1 4	- 4 4	- 5 3

16. 63	17. 50	18. 37	19. 99	20. 52
- 4 9	- 9	- 1 8	- 6 4	- 2 3

2-Digit Subtraction - Borrowing - Fill in the Blanks

Use borrowing to solve the problems below.

1. 48
  − 29
  —————
  1☐

2. 25
  − 7
  —————
  1☐

3. 60
  − ☐
  —————
  51

4. 36
  − 8
  —————
  ☐8

5. 77
  −☐9
  —————
  58

6. 60
  −☐3
  —————
  27

7. 94
  − 46
  —————
  ☐8

8. 15
  − 6
  —————
  ☐

9. ☐2
  − 9
  —————
  13

10. 30
  − 1☐
  —————
  13

11. 72
  −☐4
  —————
  48

12. 20
  −☐2
  —————
  8

13. 51
  − 16
  —————
  ☐5

14. 46
  − 9
  —————
  ☐7

15. 32
  −☐9
  —————
  13

16. 67
  − 39
  —————
  ☐8

17. 12
  − ☐
  —————
  6

18. 24
  −☐9
  —————
  5

19. 71
  −☐5
  —————
  16

20. 47
  − 19
  —————
  ☐8

Lesson 2

Subtraction Word Problems

Use subtraction to solve the problems below.

1. Selena is a good soccer player. This season she has taken 38 shots at the goal and made 6 of them. How many shots has she missed this season?

_____

2. Billy just can't stop eating cookies. He had 62 cookies in his jar. He ate 18 of them. How many cookies are left in the jar?

_____

3. Aida loves baseball. She has gone to 103 games in her life. 39 were away games. How many were home games?

_____

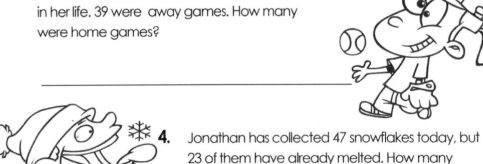

4. Jonathan has collected 47 snowflakes today, but 23 of them have already melted. How many snowflakes does Jonathan have left?

_____

Lesson 3

3-Digit Subtraction - Borrowing 1

To subtract and borrow, start with the ones column. If the bottom number is of a greater value, you have to borrow from the next column.

	Hundreds	Tens	Ones
Step 1: Any time the bottom number in a column is of greater value than the top number, you need to borrow.	7	6	3
	– 4	8	5

	Hundreds	Tens	Ones
Step 2: Borrow 10 from the next column. This reduces the 6 to 5 and increases the numbers in the first column from 3 to 13.	7	5̶6̶	13
	– 4	8	5

	Hundreds	Tens	Ones
Step 3: Now we need to borrow 10 from the hundreds column. This reduces the 7 to 6 and increases the numbers in the tens column from 5 to 15.	6̶7̶	15̶5̶	13
	– 4	8	5

	Hundreds	Tens	Ones
Step 4: Finish by subtracting the numbers in all the columns.	6̶7̶	15̶5̶	13
	– 4	8	5
	2	7	8

Use borrowing to solve the problems below.

1.
```
  289
- 134
-----
  155
```

2.
```
  412
- 389
-----
```

3.
```
  518
-  79
-----
```

4.
```
  962
- 473
-----
```

5.
```
  412
- 273
-----
```

6.
```
  652
- 386
-----
```

7.
```
  179
-  83
-----
```

8.
```
  712
- 554
-----
```

9.
```
  369
- 254
-----
```

10.
```
  811
- 632
-----
```

11.
```
  895
-  67
-----
```

12.
```
  337
- 287
-----
```

13.
```
  615
- 457
-----
```

14.
```
  906
- 687
-----
```

15.
```
  675
- 399
-----
```

3-Digit Subtraction - Borrowing 2

 Use borrowing to solve the problems below.

1. 296
  - 147

2. 472
  - 228

3. 915
  - 455

4. 371
  -   52

5. 612
  - 377

6. 501
  - 458

7. 715
  - 207

8. 185
  - 152

9. 999
  - 342

10. 307
  - 158

11. 844
  - 599

12. 199
  -   57

13. 689
  - 394

14. 472
  -   59

15. 315
  - 199

16. 578
  - 419

17. 972
  - 859

18. 572
  - 289

19. 911
  - 487

20. 308
  - 157

3-Digit Subtraction - Borrowing - Fill in the Blanks

Use borrowing to fill in the blanks below.

1. 428
  − 305
  ─────
  1□3

2. 577
  − □07
  ─────
  370

3. 671
  − 1□5
  ─────
  486

4. 780
  − 339
  ─────
  □41

5. 719
  − 45□
  ─────
  267

6. 672
  − □35
  ─────
  537

7. 517
  − 365
  ─────
  1□2

8. 217
  − 82
  ─────
  13□

9. 857
  − 369
  ─────
  4□8

10. 624
  − 29
  ─────
  □95

11. 78□
  − 345
  ─────
  440

12. 266
  − 117
  ─────
  1□9

13. 456
  − 3□5
  ─────
  141

14. 206
  − 12□
  ─────
  85

15. 367
  − 27□
  ─────
  92

16. 785
  − 316
  ─────
  46□

17. 454
  − □99
  ─────
  255

18. 720
  − 367
  ─────
  □53

19. 894
  − 176
  ─────
  7□8

20. 269
  − □56
  ─────
  113

Lesson 4

4-Digit Subtraction - Borrowing 1

 Use what you learned about borrowing to solve the problems below.

1. 6,432
    − 5,320
    ‾‾‾‾‾‾
    1,112

2. 2,675
    − 1,564
    ‾‾‾‾‾‾

3. 4,233
    −   452
    ‾‾‾‾‾‾

4. 5,428
    − 2,649
    ‾‾‾‾‾‾

5. 1,995
    −   239
    ‾‾‾‾‾‾

6. 7,321
    −   834
    ‾‾‾‾‾‾

7. 9,211
    − 1,700
    ‾‾‾‾‾‾

8. 3,946
    − 1,682
    ‾‾‾‾‾‾

9. 2,463
    − 1,939
    ‾‾‾‾‾‾

10. 8,959
    − 3,274
    ‾‾‾‾‾‾

11. 1,295
    −   968
    ‾‾‾‾‾‾

12. 9,942
    − 7,895
    ‾‾‾‾‾‾

13. 7,542
    − 2,907
    ‾‾‾‾‾‾

14. 3,649
    − 1,590
    ‾‾‾‾‾‾

15. 9,864
    − 4,389
    ‾‾‾‾‾‾

16. 3,888
    −   999
    ‾‾‾‾‾‾

17. 5,001
    − 3,547
    ‾‾‾‾‾‾

18. 1,775
    −   859
    ‾‾‾‾‾‾

19. 3,880
    − 1,125
    ‾‾‾‾‾‾

20. 9,567
    − 6,820
    ‾‾‾‾‾‾

4-Digit Subtraction - Borrowing 2

 Use what you learned about borrowing to
solve the problems below.

1. 3,291
    − 1,675
    ⎯⎯⎯⎯

2. 7,052
    − 5,894
    ⎯⎯⎯⎯

3. 1,020
    − 532
    ⎯⎯⎯⎯

4. 9,214
    − 7,580
    ⎯⎯⎯⎯

5. 2,856
    − 1,697
    ⎯⎯⎯⎯

6. 5,441
    − 2,583
    ⎯⎯⎯⎯

7. 7,654
    − 5,439
    ⎯⎯⎯⎯

8. 9,201
    − 2,550
    ⎯⎯⎯⎯

9. 6,549
    − 3,058
    ⎯⎯⎯⎯

10. 1,205
    − 317
    ⎯⎯⎯⎯

11. 4,053
    − 1,589
    ⎯⎯⎯⎯

12. 9,087
    − 4,682
    ⎯⎯⎯⎯

13. 3,001
    − 1,892
    ⎯⎯⎯⎯

14. 9,897
    − 5,432
    ⎯⎯⎯⎯

15. 6,901
    − 3,784
    ⎯⎯⎯⎯

16. 5,338
    − 2,058
    ⎯⎯⎯⎯

17. 8,071
    − 3,687
    ⎯⎯⎯⎯

18. 9,001
    − 5,592
    ⎯⎯⎯⎯

19. 4,207
    − 2,072
    ⎯⎯⎯⎯

20. 9,991
    − 3,058
    ⎯⎯⎯⎯

Lesson 5

5-Digit Subtraction - Borrowing 1

Use what you learned about borrowing to solve the problems below.

1. 62,734
   − 49,586
   13,148

2. 45,689
   − 29,875

3. 90,254
   − 67,702

4. 12,097
   − 7,850

5. 80,775
   − 24,078

6. 37,820
   − 9,507

7. 54,519
   − 20,179

8. 70,421
   − 34,219

9. 21,997
   − 1,509

10. 95,327
   − 70,587

11. 40,871
   − 27,815

12. 10,037
   − 5,871

13. 78,510
   − 40,327

14. 37,540
   − 1,058

15. 50,574
   − 27,899

16. 29,992
   − 10,871

17. 40,087
   − 21,589

18. 78,560
   − 52,278

19. 12,687
   − 11,339

20. 45,230
   − 7,854

5-Digit Subtraction - Borrowing 2

Use what you learned about borrowing to solve the problems below.

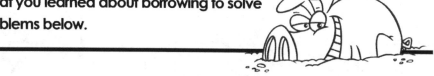

1. 13,489 – 11,792	**2.** 86,371 – 45,927

1. 13,489
  – 11,792

2. 86,371
  – 45,927

3. 50,762
  – 36,875

4. 38,792
  – 15,806

5. 21,743
  – 6,158

6. 35,309
  – 9,507

7. 98,051
  – 65,473

8. 66,259
  – 29,402

9. 32,278
  – 14,369

10. 20,897
  – 5,098

11. 55,807
  – 34,568

12. 97,051
  – 65,204

13. 65,790
  – 22,903

14. 10,854
  – 9,661

15. 77,059
  – 40,572

16. 85,220
  – 33,078

17. 36,754
  – 18,265

18. 54,587
  – 33,058

19. 63,017
  – 45,582

20. 70,000
  – 25,783

Lesson 1

Adding Decimals 1

Adding decimals is like most normal addition. You just have to remember to line up the decimals.

Hint: Decimal points always go at the end of a whole number (3 = 3.0 or 3.00)

Example: Add 2.43, 4.5 and 3		
Step 1: Line up the numbers	**Step 2:** Add zeros	**Step 3:** Find the total
2.43 4.5 + 3	2.43 4.50 + 3.00	2.43 4.50 + 3.00 9.93

Line up the numbers and solve the problems below.
Show your work in the boxes.

1: 1.21 + 2.33 + .05

```
  1.21
  2.33
+  .05
------
  3.59
```

2: 4 + 1.63 + 2.20

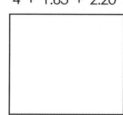

3: .24 + 4.87 + 11

4: 7.12 + 2.04 + 5

5: 9.11 + .43 + .89

6: 64 + 8.79 + 1.57

- 49 -

Adding Decimals 2

Use what you learned about adding numbers with decimals to find the totals to the questions below. Show your work in the boxes.

1:   9.34 + .44 + 6.17

2:   590 + 2.49 + 71.99

3:   .04 + 3.03 + 24.42

4:   3.18 + 2.01 + 35.78

5:   584.11 + 789.8 + .50

6:   584 + 1.29 + 36.99

7:   6.08 + 3.46 + .99

8:   15 + 37.16 + 2.09

9:   7.89 + 1.11 + 109

Lesson 2

Adding Money 1

 The rules that we learned for adding decimals is how we add money.

2.69	$2.69
+ 5.11	= + $5.11
7.80	$7.80

Find the totals below.

1. $1.40
   + $3.63
   $5.03

2. $7.18
   + $4.45

3. $2.50
   + $6.72

4. $1.15
   + $5.25

5. $9.40
   + $3.35

6. $10.45
   + $11.82

7. $20.15
   + $2.38

8. $14.05
   + $5.59

9. $6.55
   $1.47
   + $3.91

10. $2.13
   $4.75
   + $5.59

11. $1.55
   $8.09
   + $6.32

12. $2.77
   $8.59
   + $3.40

13. $17.09
   $1.99
   + $3.20

14. $10.33
   $8.95
   + $1.27

15. $18.17
   $9.49
   + $7.55

16. $12.35
   $2.78
   + $5.15

Adding Money 2

Find the totals below.

1. $9.32 + $4.13 _____ $13.45	**2.** $6.91 + $3.57	**3.** $8.10 + $2.36	**4.** $5.55 + $1.35
5. $77.02 +$62.23	**6.** $50.85 +$32.04	**7.** $29.77 +$12.75	**8.** $82.26 +$40.11

9. $16.88
  $91.05
+$53.12
	10. $55.30
	  $30.99
	+ $7.15
		11. $62.10
		   $1.99
		+ $28.50
			12. $39.03
			  $20.27
			+$51.11

13. $100.33
  $55.70
+ $7.16
	14. $555.46
	  $71.26
	+ $3.90
		15. $123.50
		  $40.49
		+ $8.17
			16. $609.99
			  $24.35
			+ $5.22

17. $759.09
  $208.99
+$177.20
	18. $405.00
	  $620.50
	+$378.99
		19. $907.89
		  $182.63
		+$330.17
			20. $365.11
			  $657.78
			+$307.40

Adding Money 3

Find the totals below.

1. $6.05
 + $4.11

2. $3.94
 + $2.29

3. $9.99
 + $7.65

4. $5.25
 + $8.39

5. $8.38
 + $9.12

6. $66.45
 +$29.82

7. $95.30
 +$12.65

8. $84.94
 + $17.05

9. $29.75
 $1.40
 + $8.97

10. $20.51
 $45.68
 + $9.42

11. $95.12
 $58.63
 +$17.08

12. $62.22
 $30.52
 +$68.67

13. $152.78
 $126.36
 + $75.11

14. $429.33
 $639.95
 +$115.27

15. $290.24
 $907.57
 +$333.03

16. $369.67
 $105.18
 + $59.07

17. $625.99
 $470.75
 +$364.23

18. $129.00
 $650.70
 +$321.33

19. $459.99
 $630.01
 +$780.40

20. $111.27
 $252.96
 +$639.57

Lesson 3

Adding Decimals Word Problems

Solve the problems below.

1. Jimmie's water gun can hold 30.08 ounces of water. Steven's water gun can hold 22.56 ounces. How many ounces of water do they have together?

_____

2. Sara walks every afternoon. On Monday she walked 2.3 miles. On Tuesday she walked 1.8 miles. On Wednesday she walked 3.1 miles. How many miles did she walk in total?

_____

3. Mickey loves to race his bike. In race one he had a finishing time of 13.38 minutes. In race two he had a finishing time of 12.58 minutes. In race three he had a finishing time of 12.32 minutes. What was his total time for all the races?

_____

4. Mary can carry 6.75 pounds of dirt in her wagon. Mark can carry 8.25 pounds in his wagon. How much dirt can they carry in total?

_____

- 54 -

Lesson 4

Rounding Decimals 1

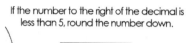

Round each decimal to the nearest whole number.

1. $9\,2.8 = \underline{9\,3}$

2. $12.5 = \underline{\hphantom{00}}$

3. $3\,3.1 = \underline{\hphantom{00}}$

4. $24.9 = \underline{\hphantom{00}}$

5. $5\,7.7 = \underline{\hphantom{00}}$

6. $65.1 = \underline{\hphantom{00}}$

7. $8\,2.5 = \underline{\hphantom{00}}$

8. $41.6 = \underline{\hphantom{00}}$

9. $6\,8.6 = \underline{\hphantom{00}}$

10. $20.4 = \underline{\hphantom{00}}$

11. $3\,4.2 = \underline{\hphantom{00}}$

12. $31.8 = \underline{\hphantom{00}}$

13. $7\,6.7 = \underline{\hphantom{00}}$

13. $72.2 = \underline{\hphantom{00}}$

15. $1\,2.3 = \underline{\hphantom{00}}$

16. $43.7 = \underline{\hphantom{00}}$

17. $4\,5.8 = \underline{\hphantom{00}}$

18. $55.9 = \underline{\hphantom{00}}$

19. $2\,1.4 = \underline{\hphantom{00}}$

20. $19.3 = \underline{\hphantom{00}}$

Rounding Decimals 2

Round each decimal to the nearest whole number.

1. $892.86 =$ _____

2. $112.51 =$ _____

3. $133.41 =$ _____

4. $24.9 =$ _____

5. $57.38 =$ _____

6. $765.12 =$ _____

7. $22.23 =$ _____

8. $341.64 =$ _____

9. $318.34 =$ _____

10. $920.48 =$ _____

11. $94.19 =$ _____

12. $31.83 =$ _____

13. $56.77 =$ _____

14. $672.26 =$ _____

15. $812.62 =$ _____

16. $543.71 =$ _____

17. $35.21 =$ _____

18. $811.95 =$ _____

19. $121.84 =$ _____

20. $698.34 =$ _____

Lesson 5

Subtracting Decimals 1

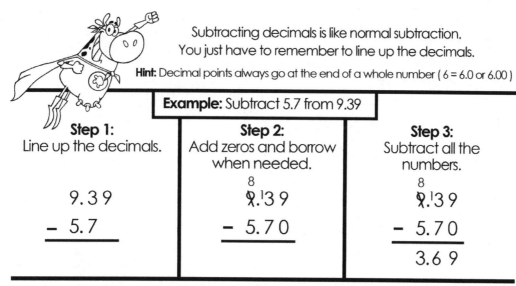

Subtracting decimals is like normal subtraction.
You just have to remember to line up the decimals.

Hint: Decimal points always go at the end of a whole number (6 = 6.0 or 6.00)

Example: Subtract 5.7 from 9.39

Step 1:
Line up the decimals.

$$
\begin{array}{r}
9.39 \\
-\ 5.7 \\
\hline
\end{array}
$$

Step 2:
Add zeros and borrow when needed.

$$
\begin{array}{r}
\overset{8}{\cancel{9}}.^{1}39 \\
-\ 5.70 \\
\hline
\end{array}
$$

Step 3:
Subtract all the numbers.

$$
\begin{array}{r}
\overset{8}{\cancel{9}}.^{1}39 \\
-\ 5.70 \\
\hline
3.69
\end{array}
$$

Line up the numbers and solve the problems below.
Show your work in the boxes.

---

1. 6.05 - 3.89

$$
\begin{array}{r}
6.05 \\
-\ 3.89 \\
\hline
2.16
\end{array}
$$

2. 48.27 - 13.65

3. 8.55 - 3.9

4. 331 - 4.72

5. 902.22 - 47.79

6. 75.5 - 6.51

Subtracting Decimals 2

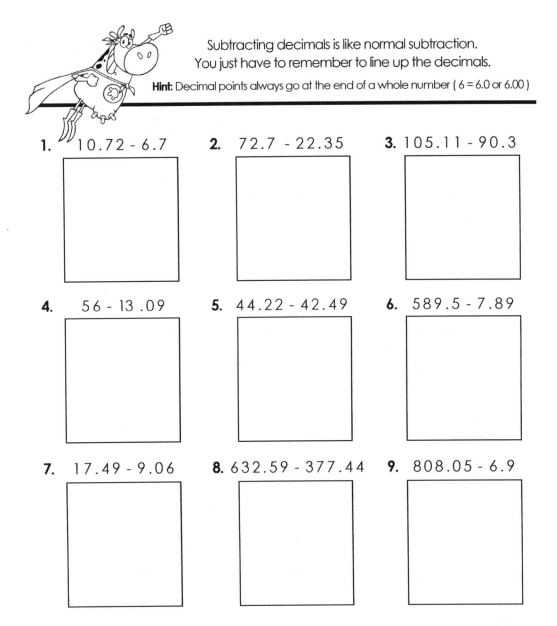

Subtracting decimals is like normal subtraction.
You just have to remember to line up the decimals.

Hint: Decimal points always go at the end of a whole number (6 = 6.0 or 6.00)

1. 10.72 - 6.7

2. 72.7 - 22.35

3. 105.11 - 90.3

4. 56 - 13 .09

5. 44.22 - 42.49

6. 589.5 - 7.89

7. 17.49 - 9.06

8. 632.59 - 377.44

9. 808.05 - 6.9

Lesson 6

Subtracting Money 1

Now that you know how to subtract decimals, use what you learned to answer these money problems.

$$
\begin{array}{r}
6.89 \\
- \quad 4.32 \\
\hline
2.57
\end{array}
\quad = \quad
\begin{array}{r}
\$6.89 \\
- \quad \$4.32 \\
\hline
\$2.57
\end{array}
$$

Subtract the amounts below.

1. $\begin{array}{r} \$4.58 \\ - \ \$2.11 \\ \hline \$2.47 \end{array}$

2. $\begin{array}{r} \$8.49 \\ - \ \$5.35 \\ \hline \end{array}$

3. $\begin{array}{r} \$6.50 \\ - \ \$3.32 \\ \hline \end{array}$

4. $\begin{array}{r} \$9.75 \\ - \ \$7.89 \\ \hline \end{array}$

5. $\begin{array}{r} \$9.90 \\ - \ \$8.75 \\ \hline \end{array}$

6. $\begin{array}{r} \$2.93 \\ - \ \$1.08 \\ \hline \end{array}$

7. $\begin{array}{r} \$6.15 \\ - \ \$2.38 \\ \hline \end{array}$

8. $\begin{array}{r} \$7.38 \\ - \ \$5.08 \\ \hline \end{array}$

9. $\begin{array}{r} \$4.15 \\ - \ \$1.02 \\ \hline \end{array}$

10. $\begin{array}{r} \$5.65 \\ - \ \$2.36 \\ \hline \end{array}$

11. $\begin{array}{r} \$3.46 \\ - \ \$3.07 \\ \hline \end{array}$

12. $\begin{array}{r} \$9.15 \\ - \ \$6.10 \\ \hline \end{array}$

13. $\begin{array}{r} \$13.04 \\ - \ \$8.25 \\ \hline \end{array}$

14. $\begin{array}{r} \$31.35 \\ - \ \$9.07 \\ \hline \end{array}$

15. $\begin{array}{r} \$15.89 \\ - \ \$2.35 \\ \hline \end{array}$

16. $\begin{array}{r} \$17.38 \\ - \ \$6.40 \\ \hline \end{array}$

17. $\begin{array}{r} \$16.82 \\ - \ \$9.05 \\ \hline \end{array}$

18. $\begin{array}{r} \$21.93 \\ - \ \$7.08 \\ \hline \end{array}$

19. $\begin{array}{r} \$10.15 \\ - \ \$2.38 \\ \hline \end{array}$

20. $\begin{array}{r} \$20.00 \\ - \$10.99 \\ \hline \end{array}$

Subtracting Money 2

Subtract the amounts below.

1. $10.13
    − $2.29

2. $25.55
    − $5.02

3. $17.89
    − $3.39

4. $20.15
    − $7.09

5. $45.77
    − $15.36

6. $23.01
    − $17.99

7. $39.50
    − $27.28

8. $26.55
    − $11.17

9. $58.37
    − $49.99

10. $79.44
    − $60.76

11. $62.08
    − $34.13

12. $95.35
    − $17.37

13. $100.04
    − $68.68

14. $216.42
    − $84.36

15. $199.55
    − $35.23

16. $956.11
    − $25.71

17. $209.44
    − $155.88

18. $356.77
    − $208.05

19. $589.33
    − $199.07

20. $250.99
    − $217.95

Lesson 7

Subtracting Decimals Word Problems

Use subtraction to solve the problems below.

1. Pete wants a new teddy bear. His mom is going to help him buy one. A new bear costs $19.50. Pete has $7.32. How much money does he need to get from mom?

_____

2. Tammy wants a new jump rope. She has $3.78. The jump rope costs $6.99. How much more money does she need?

_____

3. Randy and John want a new toy truck. The toy truck costs $13.75. Randy has $4.15 and John has $6.42. How much more money do they need?

_____

4. Eric sold his old pogo stick for $5.89. A new one costs $35.99. How much more money does Eric need?

_____

Lesson 1

Multiplication

Multiplication Table

x	1	2	3	4	5	6	7	8	9	10
1	1	2	3	4	5	6	7	8	9	10
2	2	4	6	8	10	12	14	16	18	20
3	3	6	9	12	15	18	21	24	27	30
4	4	8	12	16	20	24	28	32	36	40
5	5	10	15	20	25	30	35	40	45	50
6	6	12	18	24	30	36	42	48	54	60
7	7	14	21	28	35	42	49	56	63	70
8	8	16	24	32	40	48	56	64	72	80
9	9	18	27	36	45	54	63	72	81	90
10	10	20	30	40	50	60	70	80	90	100

This is a **multiplication table**.
It shows how numbers multiply together.
The numbers in the **top row** multiply
by the numbers in the **left side row**.
Match up the rows to get your answer.

Lesson 2

Multiplication Tables 1

X	1	2	3
1	1	2	3
2	2	4	6

This is a multiplication table. Multiply the numbers in the top row by the numbers in the side row.

1.

X	1	2	3	4	5
6					
7					
8					

2.

X	7	8	9
4			
5			
6			
7			
8			

3.

X	9	10	11
7			
8			
9			
10			
11			

4.

X	2	3	4	5	6
20					
25					
27					

Lesson 3

Multiplying 1-Digit Numbers by 2-Digit Numbers

To multiply a one-digit number by a two-digit number, start in the ones place and then use basic multiplication rules.

	Tens	Ones
Step 1: Multiply the numbers in the ones place	4	3 ↑
	x	2
		6

	Tens	Ones
Step 2: Multiply the numbers in the tens place	4	3
	x	2
	8	6

Solve the problems below.

1. 2 4
   x 2
   ———
   4 8

2. 3 1
   x 3
   ———

3. 4 3
   x 2
   ———

4. 1 1
   x 7
   ———

5. 1 1
   x 5
   ———

6. 4 4
   x 2
   ———

7. 1 1
   x 9
   ———

8. 1 8
   x 1
   ———

9. 2 1
   x 4
   ———

10. 2 2
    x 3
    ———

Lesson 4

Multiplying by 10s

Multiplying by ten is just like regular two-digit number multiplication, but there is just one extra step. You bring the zero down first; this adds it to the end of the number.

Hundreds	Tens	Ones
	5	4
x	1	0
		[0]

Hundreds	Tens	Ones
	5	4
x	1	0
	[4]	0

Hundreds	Tens	Ones
	5	4
x	1	0
[5]	4	0

Solve the problems below.

1.
$$\begin{array}{r} 26 \\ \times\ 10 \\ \hline 260 \end{array}$$

2.
$$\begin{array}{r} 71 \\ \times\ 10 \\ \hline \end{array}$$

3.
$$\begin{array}{r} 67 \\ \times\ 10 \\ \hline \end{array}$$

4.
$$\begin{array}{r} 22 \\ \times\ 10 \\ \hline \end{array}$$

5.
$$\begin{array}{r} 38 \\ \times\ 10 \\ \hline \end{array}$$

6.
$$\begin{array}{r} 84 \\ \times\ 10 \\ \hline \end{array}$$

7.
$$\begin{array}{r} 19 \\ \times\ 10 \\ \hline \end{array}$$

8.
$$\begin{array}{r} 18 \\ \times\ 10 \\ \hline \end{array}$$

9.
$$\begin{array}{r} 94 \\ \times\ 10 \\ \hline \end{array}$$

10.
$$\begin{array}{r} 29 \\ \times\ 10 \\ \hline \end{array}$$

Multiplying by 10s 2

Multiplying by ten is just like regular two-digit multiplication, but there is just one extra step. You bring the zero down first; this adds it to the end of the number.

Solve the problems below by multiplying the numbers by ten.

---

1. 4 4
   x 1 0

2. 8 9
   x 2 0

3. 5 2
   x 5 0

4. 1 3
   x 9 0

5. 4 8
   x 3 0

6. 4 9
   x 2 0

7. 1 8
   x 1 0

8. 3 3
   x 8 0

9. 9 2
   x 5 0

10. 5 7
    x 7 0

11. 6 7
    x 1 0

12. 2 1
    x 6 0

13. 2 7
    x 1 0

14. 7 5
    x 9 0

15. 5 0
    x 3 0

16. 6 6
    x 2 0

17. 8 2
    x 1 0

18. 5 5
    x 3 0

19. 4 5
    x 5 0

20. 6 1
    x 9 0

Multiplying by 10 3

 Multiplying by ten is just like regular two-digit multiplication, but there is just one extra step. You bring the zero down first; this adds it to the end of the number.

Solve the problems below by filling in the blanks.

1. 82 x 10 = <u>820</u>   2. 59 x 10 = _____

3. 36 x 10 = _____   4. 91 x 10 = _____

5. 27 x 10 = _____   6. 60 x 10 = _____

7. 10 x 95 = _____   8. 10 x 89 = _____

9. 10 x 43 = _____   10. 10 x 27 = _____

11. 10 x 56 = _____   12. 10 x 39 = _____

13. _____ x 10 = 750   14. 12 x _____ = 120

15. 10 x _____ = 880   16. _____ x 10 = 620

17. _____ x 10 = 590   18. 10 x _____ = 10

Lesson 5

Multiplying 1-Digit Numbers by 2-Digit Numbers - Regrouping

To multiply a one-digit number by a two-digit number with regrouping, start in the ones place and then use basic multiplication rules. When the number equals ten or more, the first digit carries over to the next spot. This is called **regrouping**.

	Hundreds	Tens	Ones
Step 1: Multiply the numbers in the ones column and carry the first digit over to the tens column.		2 4	7 ↑ 3
	x		
			[1]

$3 \times 7 = 21$

	Hundreds	Tens	Ones
Step 2: Multiply the digit in at the bottom of the ones column by the digit in the tens column and add the regrouped number.		2 + 4	7 3
	x		
		[4]	1

$4 \times 3 = 12$ Then $12 + 2 = 14$

	Hundreds	Tens	Ones
Step 3: The one then carries over to the hundreds place.		2 4	7 3
	x		
	[1]	4	1

Answer $= 141$

Solve the problems below.

1.   4 6
  x   2
    9 2

2.   5 8
  x   7

3.   4 3
  x   4

4.   8 7
  x   3

5.   3 6
  x   5

6.   4 4
  x   5

7.   3 2
  x   9

8.   5 5
  x   9

9.   9 9
  x   2

10.   5 9
  x   6

Multiplying 1-Digit numbers by 2-Digit numbers - Regrouping 2

To multiply a one-digit number by a two-digit number with regrouping, start in the ones place and then use basic multiplication rules. When the number equals ten or more the first digit carries over to the next spot. This is called **regrouping**.

Solve the problems below.

1. 28
   x 3

2. 75
   x 2

3. 13
   x 4

4. 62
   x 9

5. 99
   x 2

6. 85
   x 5

7. 26
   x 7

8. 44
   x 4

9. 96
   x 3

10. 57
    x 6

11. 72
    x 2

12. 33
    x 8

13. 82
    x 5

14. 29
    x 9

15. 66
    x 4

16. 59
    x 4

17. 26
    x 9

18. 54
    x 7

19. 95
    x 5

20. 46
    x 6

Lesson 6

Multiplying 1-Digit Numbers by 3-Digit Numbers - Regrouping

To multiply a one-digit number by a three-digit number, start in the ones place and then use basic multiplication rules.

	Hundreds	Tens	Ones
Step 1: First multiply the top digit in the ones column by the bottom digit in the ones column.	2	3	3 ˣ
x			3
			9

$3 \times 3 = 9$

	Hundreds	Tens	Ones
Step 2: Next multiply the digit in the tens column by the bottom digit in the ones column.	2	3	3
x			3
		9	9

$3 \times 3 = 9$

	Hundreds	Tens	Ones
Step 3: Next multiply the digit in the hundreds column by the bottom digit in the ones column.	2	3	3
x			3
	6	9	9

$2 \times 3 = 6$

Answer = 699

Solve the problems below.

1. 1 4 2
   x   2
  ———
   2 8 4

2. 2 2 1
   x   3
  ———

3. 3 4 1
   x   2
  ———

4. 1 2 1
   x   4
  ———

5. 6 9 8
   x   1
  ———

6. 2 1 2
   x   4
  ———

7. 1 3 2
   x   3
  ———

8. 2 3 3
   x   2
  ———

9. 2 3 2
   x   3
  ———

10. 1 4 1
    x   2
   ———

11. 2 1 2
    x   3
   ———

12. 1 1 2
    x   3
   ———

Multiplying 1-Digit numbers by 3-Digit numbers - Regrouping 2

To multiply a one-digit number by a three-digit number, start in the ones place and then use basic multiplication rules. Dont forget to use the regrouping rules you learned in the previous sections.

Solve the problems below.

1. 6 5 1
    x   2

2. 2 2 1
    x   3

3. 3 4 1
    x   5

4. 4 3 3
    x   4

5. 6 9 8
    x   9

6. 2 1 2
    x   4

7. 1 3 2
    x   3

8. 2 3 3
    x   8

9. 2 3 2
    x   9

10. 5 4 9
    x   2

11. 6 8 9
    x   7

12. 5 9 9
    x   5

13. 9 8 6
    x   8

14. 1 2 3
    x   6

15. 9 7 7
    x   4

16. 2 2 2
    x   5

17. 6 8 5
    x   4

18. 3 0 4
    x   8

19. 9 6 0
    x   9

20. 7 9 5
    x   2

Lesson 7

Multiplying 2-Digit numbers by 3-Digit numbers - Regrouping

To multiply a two-digit number by a two-digit number, start in the ones place and then use basic multiplication and addition rules. Dont forget to use what you learned about regrouping.

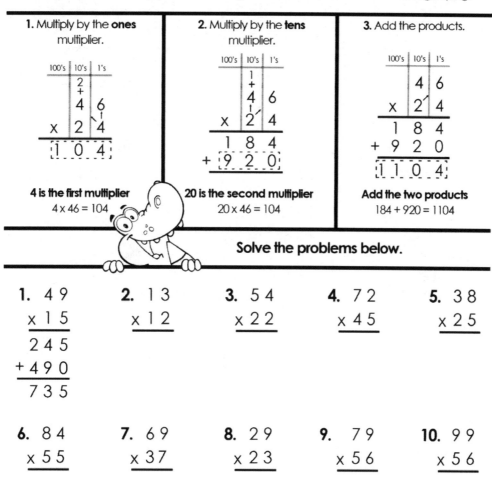

1. Multiply by the **ones** multiplier.	2. Multiply by the **tens** multiplier.	3. Add the products.
4 is the first multiplier 4 x 46 = 104	**20 is the second multiplier** 20 x 46 = 104	**Add the two products** 184 + 920 = 1104

Solve the problems below.

1. 49
    x 1 5
    ‾‾‾‾‾
    2 4 5
    + 4 9 0
    ‾‾‾‾‾
    7 3 5

2. 1 3
    x 1 2
    ‾‾‾‾‾

3. 5 4
    x 2 2
    ‾‾‾‾‾

4. 7 2
    x 4 5
    ‾‾‾‾‾

5. 3 8
    x 2 5
    ‾‾‾‾‾

6. 8 4
    x 5 5
    ‾‾‾‾‾

7. 6 9
    x 3 7
    ‾‾‾‾‾

8. 2 9
    x 2 3
    ‾‾‾‾‾

9. 7 9
    x 5 6
    ‾‾‾‾‾

10. 9 9
    x 5 6
    ‾‾‾‾‾

Multiplying 2-Digit numbers by 3-Digit numbers - Regrouping 2

Solve the problems below.

1. 67
    x 49

2. 24
    x 15

3. 49
    x 36

4. 29
    x 27

5. 44
    x 39

6. 84
    x 60

7. 66
    x 34

8. 87
    x 11

9. 99
    x 49

10. 70
    x 59

11. 39
    x 27

12. 24
    x 17

13. 86
    x 37

14. 11
    x 83

15. 97
    x 57

16. 55
    x 90

17. 75
    x 22

18. 68
    x 43

19. 92
    x 37

20. 19
    x 26

Lesson 1

Division

- Division is a way to find out how many times one number is counted in another number.

- The ÷ sign means "divided by".

- Another way to divide is to use $\overline{)}$.

- The dividend is the larger number that is divided by the smaller number, the divisor.

- The answer of a division problem is called the quotient.

÷ means divide

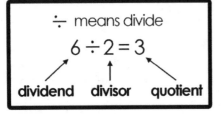

- 6 ÷ 2 = 3 is read "6 divided by 2 is equal to 3".

- In 6 ÷ 2 = 3, the divisor is 2, the dividend is 6 and the quotient is 3.

$\overline{)}$ means divide

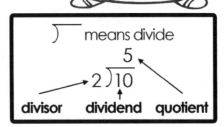

- $2\overline{)10}$ is read "10 divided by 2 is equal to 5".

- In $2\overline{)10}$, the divisor is 2, the dividend is 10 and the quotient is 5.

Lesson 2

Basic Division

Divide these problems.

1. $7\overline{)21}$ $\overset{3}{}$

2. $6\overline{)48}$

3. $2\overline{)12}$

4. $7\overline{)28}$

5. $4\overline{)36}$

6. $3\overline{)21}$

7. $7\overline{)21}$

8. $5\overline{)40}$

9. $5\overline{)15}$

10. $2\overline{)6}$

11. $8\overline{)72}$

12. $10\overline{)100}$

13. $8\overline{)32}$

14. $5\overline{)25}$

15. $5\overline{)5}$

16. $8\overline{)88}$

17. $8\overline{)56}$

18. $5\overline{)75}$

19. $3\overline{)9}$

20. $4\overline{)32}$

Lesson 3

Division with Remainders 1

- Sometimes groups of objects or numbers cannot be divided into equal groups.
- The number left over in a division problem is called the remainder.
- The remainder must be smaller than the divisor.

If we divide 13 🍎 into groups of 5, you get 2 equal groups

and 3 🍎 left over. These are the **remainders**.

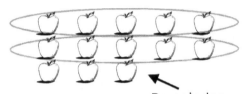

This is how you write it out. ➜

$$
\begin{array}{r}
2\,r\,3 \\
5\,\overline{)\,13} \\
-10 \\
\hline
3
\end{array}
$$

Remainders

Divide these problems. Some may not have remainders.

---

1. $\begin{array}{r} 2\,r\,2 \\ 3\,\overline{)\,8} \\ -6 \\ \hline 2 \end{array}$

2. $7\,\overline{)\,35}$

3. $6\,\overline{)\,25}$

4. $8\,\overline{)\,39}$

5. $5\,\overline{)\,52}$

6. $9\,\overline{)\,85}$

7. $5\,\overline{)\,61}$

8. $3\,\overline{)\,43}$

Division with Remainders 2

Divide these problems. Some may not have remainders.

1. $2\overline{)9}$ 2. $6\overline{)15}$ 3. $2\overline{)33}$

4. $3\overline{)15}$ 5. $5\overline{)27}$ 6. $9\overline{)44}$

7. $9\overline{)58}$ 8. $7\overline{)32}$ 9. $6\overline{)40}$

10. $2\overline{)77}$ 11. $8\overline{)99}$ 12. $2\overline{)61}$

13. $8\overline{)66}$ 14. $5\overline{)62}$ 15. $8\overline{)49}$

Lesson 4

Division - Fill in the Blanks

Use division to fill in the boxes on the problems below.

1. $4\overline{)36}$ 9

2. $6\overline{)\ }$ 9

3. $4\overline{)\ }$ 15

4. $5\overline{)\ }$ 20

5. $3\overline{)\ }$ 2

6. $7\overline{)\ }$ 7

7. $2\overline{)\ }$ 5

8. $9\overline{)\ }$ 5

9. $8\overline{)\ }$ 8

10. $9\overline{)\ }$ 32

11. $7\overline{)\ }$ 9

12. $3\overline{)\ }$ 11

13. $6\overline{)\ }$ 9

14. $4\overline{)\ }$ 6

Division - Fill in the Blanks 2

Use division to fill in the boxes on the problems below.

1. $8 \overline{)48}$ 6

2. $\boxed{} \overline{)77}$ 7

3. $\boxed{} \overline{)35}$ 15

4. $\boxed{} \overline{)12}$ 2

5. $\boxed{} \overline{)45}$ 9

6. $\boxed{} \overline{)63}$ 5

7. $\boxed{} \overline{)28}$ 7

8. $\boxed{} \overline{)63}$ 7

9. $\boxed{} \overline{)32}$ 8

10. $\boxed{} \overline{)72}$ 12

11. $\boxed{} \overline{)36}$ 6

12. $\boxed{} \overline{)98}$ 11

13. $\boxed{} \overline{)36}$ 4

14. $\boxed{} \overline{)54}$ 6

Lesson 5

Division Word Problems

Use division to solve the problems below.

1. Rachel bought three pairs of ballet shoes for $99. What is the cost of each pair of shoes?

_____

2. Charlie has 21 kids in his class. If he divides the kids into 3 groups how many kids will be in each group?

_____

3. Sara loves her dolls; she has 12 of them. If she divides them into groups of 4, how many dolls will be in each group?

_____

4. Harry has 72 toy trucks and cars. If he divides them into groups of 8, how many cars and trucks will be in each group?

_____

Lesson 6

2-Digit Quotients 1

Estimate	Divide the tens	Bring down the ones and repeat the steps.	The answer is: **23 r 3**
2 $4\overline{)95}$ Take a look at the first digit. Estimate how many times 4 will go into 9 without going over the number.	2 $4\overline{)95}$ -8 1 4 can go into 9 twice. Multiply 4 x 2 and get 8. Subtract the 8 from 9 leaving 1.	23 $4\overline{)95}$ $-8\downarrow$ 15 -12 3 Bring down the 5 from the one's column and repeat the steps. **The remainder is 3**	Remember these steps: 1. Divide 2. Multiply 3. Subtract 4. Bring down Repeat these steps until there are no more digits to bring down.

Divide these problems. Some may not have remainders.

1. $\begin{array}{r} 28\,r\,1 \\ 2\overline{)57} \\ -4 \\ \hline 17 \\ -16 \\ \hline 1 \end{array}$ **2.** $3\overline{)72}$ **3.** $4\overline{)65}$ **4.** $3\overline{)86}$

5. $2\overline{)37}$ **6.** $7\overline{)93}$ **7.** $5\overline{)73}$ **8.** $7\overline{)98}$

2-Digit Quotients 2

Divide these problems. Some may not have remainders.

1. 6)98   2. 3)65   3. 2)85   4. 4)99

5. 3)54   6. 6)77   7. 6)97   8. 2)59

9. 3)76   10. 2)46   11. 6)89   12. 3)44

Lesson 7

Dividing 3-Digit Numbers 1

When dividing a three-digit number by a two-digit number, the quotient may have two or three digits. Here are some examples:

Estimate	Divide	Estimate	Divide
200 3)719	239 r 2 3)719 - 6 11 - 9 29 - 27 2	70 3)235	78 r 1 3)235 - 21 25 - 24 1

1. Divide
2. Multiply
3. Subtract
4. Compare
5. Bring down

Repeat the steps as needed

1. Divide
2. Multiply
3. Subtract
4. Compare
5. Bring down

Repeat the steps as needed

Divide these problems. Some may not have remainders.

1.
```
    246 r 3
  4)987
   - 8
    18
   -16
    27
   - 24
     3
```

2. 6)297

3. 2)592

4. 3)769

5. 4)867

6. 5)934

Dividing 3-Digit Numbers 2

Divide these problems. Some may not have remainders.

1. $6\overline{)987}$ 2. $5\overline{)857}$ 3. $4\overline{)827}$

4. $4\overline{)359}$ 5. $9\overline{)289}$ 6. $2\overline{)764}$ 7. $7\overline{)357}$

8. $2\overline{)923}$ 9. $4\overline{)577}$ 10. $9\overline{)956}$ 11. $5\overline{)234}$

12. $8\overline{)649}$ 13. $7\overline{)937}$ 14. $3\overline{)899}$ 15. $4\overline{)521}$

Lesson 8

Averaging 1

An average is found by adding two or more quantities together and dividing by the number of quantities.

Step 1: Find the sum of the quantities $\longrightarrow$ $35 + 15 + 10 = 60$

Step 2: Divide by the number of quantities $\longrightarrow$ $60 \div 3 = \boxed{20}$

Work the problems out. Find the average of each set of numbers.

1. $6, 12, 15 = \underline{\ 11\ }$

$$\begin{array}{r} 6 \\ 12 \\ +\ 15 \\ \hline 33 \div 3 = \boxed{11} \end{array}$$

2. $1, 13, 9, 65 = \underline{\hspace{1cm}}$

3. $2, 7, 11, 12 = \underline{\hspace{1cm}}$

4. $48, 23, 28 = \underline{\hspace{1cm}}$

5. $2, 29, 35, 18 = \underline{\hspace{1cm}}$

6. $9, 33, 17, 29 = \underline{\hspace{1cm}}$

Averaging 2

Find the average of each set of numbers.
Work the problems out.

1. 10, 62, 24 = _____

2. 28, 72, 44 = _____

3. 13, 51, 87, 65 = _____

4. 25, 78, 92, 13 = _____

5. 63, 32, 72, 90, 98 = _____

6. 100, 59, 87, 33, 21 = _____

Lesson 9

Averaging Word Problems

Write out each averaging problem and solve.

1. Jamie wants to know her average test score in math class. On her 4 tests she scored 79, 86, 92 and 80. What is her average test score?

_____

2. Steven scored 17, 16, 19, 27, 21 points in 5 games. How many points did he average?

_____

3. Kenny is good at video games. He played the game 6 times. He scored 128, 58, 166, 164, 212 and 72. What is his average score?

_____

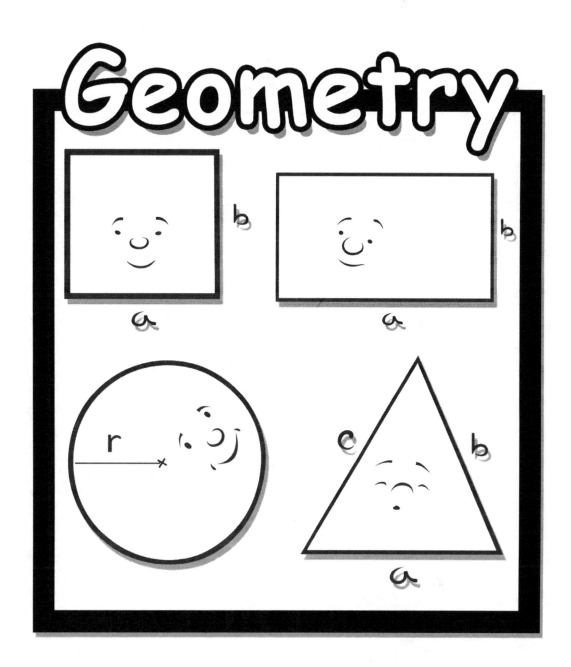

Lesson 1

Flat Shapes

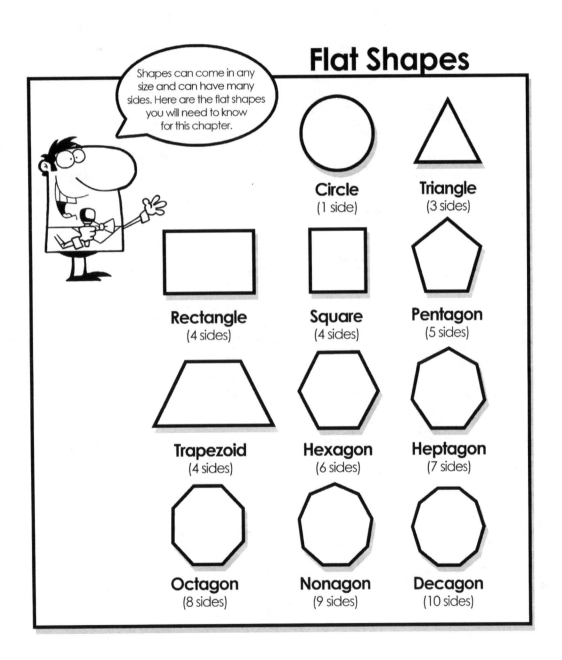

Identifying Flat Shapes

Write the number of sides in each box below.
Write the name of each shape in the blanks.

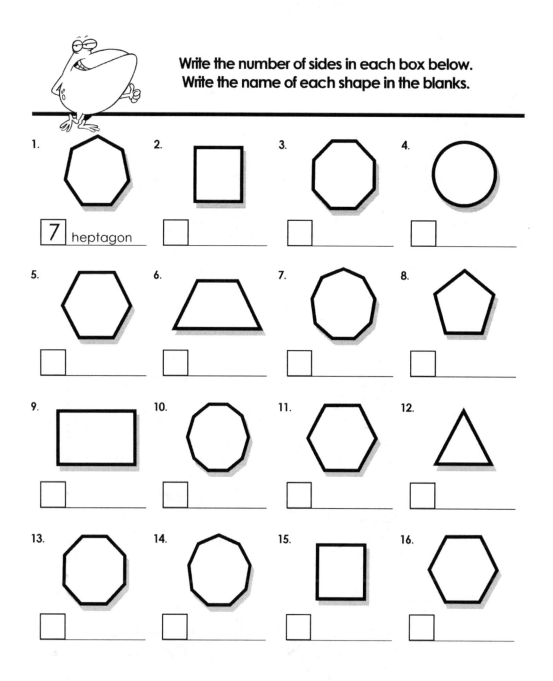

1.

7 heptagon

2.

3.

4.

5.

6.

7.

8.

9.

10.

11.

12.

13.

14.

15.

16.

Lesson 2

Solid Shape

Solid Shapes

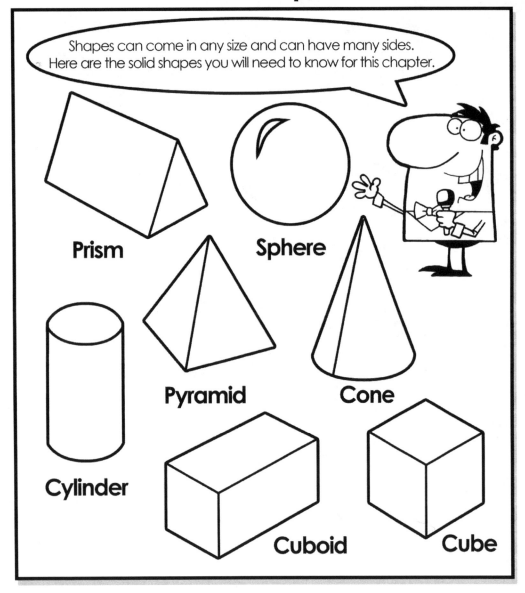

Identifying Solid Shape

Identify each shape below and write the
names in the blanks.

1.

cube

2.

_____

3.

_____

4.

_____

5.

_____

6.

_____

7.

_____

8.

_____

9.

_____

10.

_____

11.

_____

12.

_____

13.
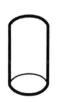
_____

14.

_____

15.

_____

16.

_____

Lesson 3

Identifying Triangles

Triangles can come in many shapes. Here are some examples.

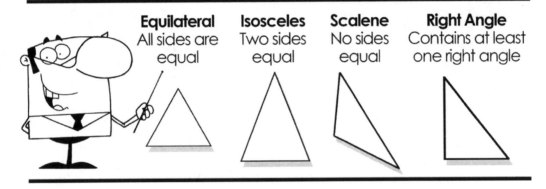

| **Equilateral** All sides are equal | **Isosceles** Two sides equal | **Scalene** No sides equal | **Right Angle** Contains at least one right angle |

Name each triangle as an **equilateral**, **isosceles**, **scalene** or **right** triangle.

1.

isosceles

2.

_____

3.

_____

4.

_____

5.

_____

6.

_____

7.

_____

8.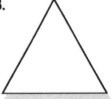

_____

Lesson 4

Identifying Points, Lines and Rays

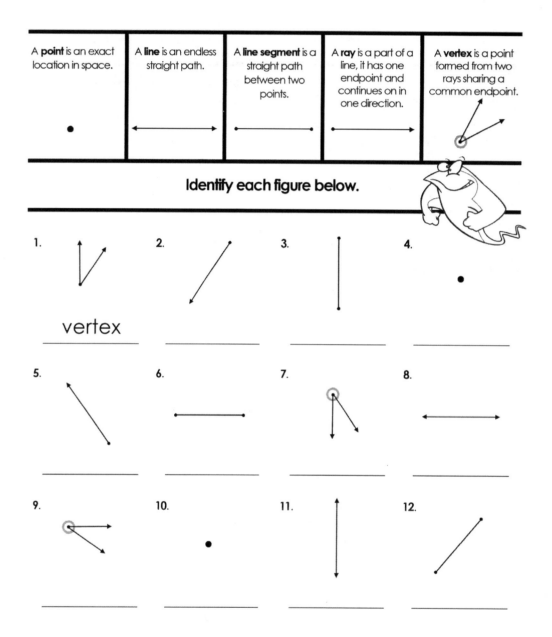

| A **point** is an exact location in space. | A **line** is an endless straight path. | A **line segment** is a straight path between two points. | A **ray** is a part of a line, it has one endpoint and continues on in one direction. | A **vertex** is a point formed from two rays sharing a common endpoint. |

Identify each figure below.

1.

vertex
_____

2.

_____

3.

_____

4.

_____

5.

_____

6.

_____

7.

_____

8.

_____

9.

_____

10.

_____

11.

_____

12.

_____

Lesson 5

Identifying Parallel and Perpendicular Lines

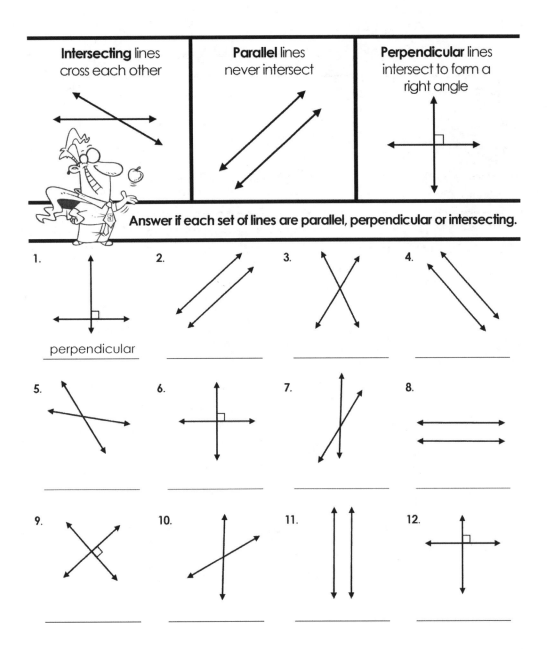

Intersecting lines cross each other

Parallel lines never intersect

Perpendicular lines intersect to form a right angle

Answer if each set of lines are parallel, perpendicular or intersecting.

1. perpendicular

2. _____

3. _____

4. _____

5. _____

6. _____

7. _____

8. _____

9. _____

10. _____

11. _____

12. _____

Lesson 6

Identifying Angles

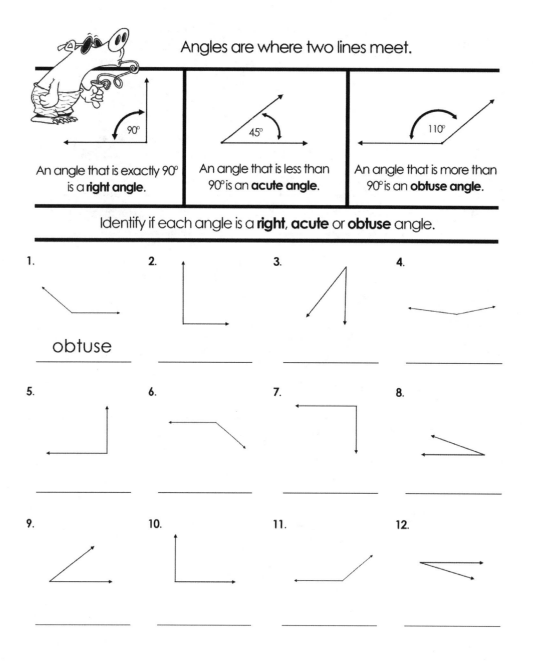

Angles are where two lines meet.

An angle that is exactly 90° is a **right angle**.

An angle that is less than 90° is an **acute angle**.

An angle that is more than 90° is an **obtuse angle**.

Identify if each angle is a **right**, **acute** or **obtuse** angle.

1. obtuse

2.

3.

4.

5.

6.

7.

8.

9.

10.

11.

12.

- 98 -

Lesson 7

Finding Area

Area is the measurement of a shape's surface area.
To find the **area** of a shape, multiply the length by the width.

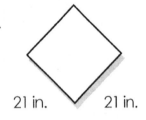

24 ft.

8 ft.

Area = 24 ft. x 8 ft. = 192 ft.
Area = 192 sq. ft.

Find the area of each shape. Write the problem out.

1. 6 in.

6 in.

$6 \times 6 = 36$ sq. in.

2. 3 ft.

12 ft.

_____

3.

21 in. 21 in.

_____

4. 4 ft.

25 ft.

_____

5.

12 yd. 12 yd.

_____

6. 9 in.

9 in.

_____

Lesson 8

Finding Perimeter 1

Perimeter is the distance around an object.
Find the perimeter of each object by adding all the sides.

12 in.

10 in.   **10** in.   **Perimeter** = 12 in. + 12 in. + 10 in. + 10 in.

Perimeter = 44 in.

12 in.

Find the perimeter of each shape. Write the problem out.

1.
20 yd.

50 yd.   50 yd.

20 yd.

$20 + 50 + 20 + 50 = 140$yd.

2.
2 ft.

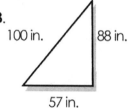

10 ft.   8 ft.

5 ft.

_____

3.

100 in.   88 in.

57 in.

_____

4.
20 ft.

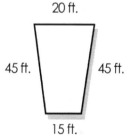

45 ft.   45 ft.

15 ft.

_____

5.
34 in.

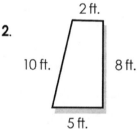

37 in.   75 in.

29 in.

_____

6.
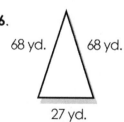

68 yd.   68 yd.

27 yd.

_____

Finding Perimeter 2

Find the perimeter of each shape.
Write the problem out.

1.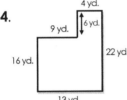

6 yd.
8 yd.
4 yd.

8 + 4 + 6 = 18yd.

2.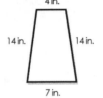

4 in.
14 in.   14 in.
7 in.

_____

3.

7 ft.
7 ft.   5 ft.
5 ft.   7 ft.
7 ft.

_____

4.

4 yd.
9 yd.   6 yd.
16 yd.   22 yd.
13 yd.

_____

5.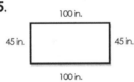

100 in.
45 in.   45 in.
100 in.

_____

6.

88 ft.   88 ft.
40 ft.

_____

7.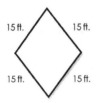

15 ft.   15 ft.
15 ft.   15 ft.

_____

8.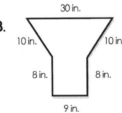

30 in.
10 in.   10 in.
8 in.   8 in.
9 in.

_____

9.

9 yd.
8 yd.   3 yd.   4 yd.
4 yd.   3 yd.   8 yd.
9 yd.

_____

Lesson 9

Understanding Volume 1

This cube is 1 ft long, 1 ft high and 1 ft wide. It has a volume of 1 cubic foot. (1ft^3).

1 ft.
1 ft.
1 ft.

When 4 of these cubes are put together, the new shape has a volume of 4 ft^3.

Find the volume of the shapes below.

1.

___3___ ft^3

2.

_____ ft^3

3.

_____ ft^3

4.

_____ ft^3

5.

_____ ft^3

6.

_____ ft^3

7.

_____ ft^3

8.

_____ ft^3

9.

_____ ft^3

Understanding Volume 2

Volume is the number of cubic units that can fit into a shape.
To find volume, count the cubes or multiply length
times width times height. *(L x W x H = volume)*

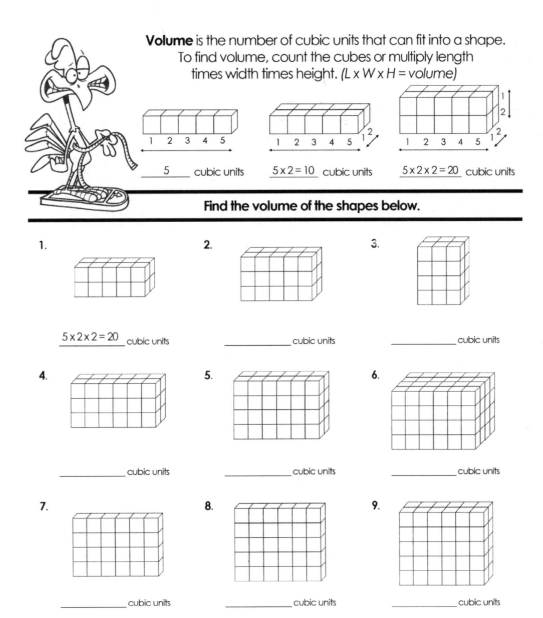

_____5_____ cubic units   5 x 2 = 10 cubic units   5 x 2 x 2 = 20 cubic units

Find the volume of the shapes below.

1.

5 x 2 x 2 = 20 cubic units

2.

_____ cubic units

3.

_____ cubic units

4.

_____ cubic units

5.

_____ cubic units

6.

_____ cubic units

7.

_____ cubic units

8.

_____ cubic units

9.

_____ cubic units

Understanding Volume 3

Volume is the number of cubic units that can fit into a shape. To find volume, multiply length times width times height.
(L x W x H = volume)

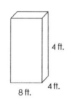

11 ft. 2 ft. 2 ft.

11 x 2 x 2 = 44 cubic feet

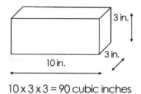

3 in. 10 in. 3 in.

10 x 3 x 3 = 90 cubic inches

Find the volume of the shapes below.

1.

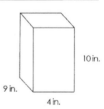

20 in. 5 in. 5 in.

$20 \times 5 \times 5 = 500 \text{ in.}^3$

2.

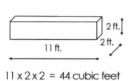

4 ft. 8 ft. 4 ft.

_____

3.

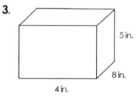

5 in. 8 in. 4 in.

_____

4.

16 ft. 5 ft. 9 ft.

_____

5.

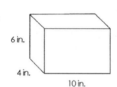

6 in. 4 in. 10 in.

_____

6.

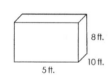

8 ft. 10 ft. 5 ft.

_____

7.

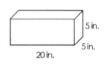

10 in. 9 in. 4 in.

_____

8.

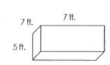

7 ft. 7 ft. 5 ft.

_____

9.

3 in. 6 in. 9 in.

_____

Lesson 1

Measurement

Capacity	Length	Weight
1 gallon = 8 pints	1 foot = 12 inches	1 pound = 16 ounces
1 gallon = 4 quarts	1 yard = 3 feet	1 ton = 2000 pounds
1 gallon = 16 cups	1 yard = 36 inches	1 ton = 32000 ounces
1 gallon = 128 fluid ounces	1 mile = 5280 feet	
1 quart = 4 cups	1 mile = 1760 yards	
1 quart = 2 pints		
1 pint = 2 cups		
1 cup = 8 fluid ounces		
1 pint = 16 fluid ounces		

Here are the measurements for **capacity**, **length** and **weight** you will need to know for this chapter.

Lesson 2

Ounces, Pounds and Tons Word Problems

Circle the correct answer for each question.

1. Lilly has grown a lot over the summer. How much does she weigh now?

   (60 pounds)   60 ounces   60 tons

2. Dad's new truck is very heavy; how much does it weigh?

   2 pounds   2 ounces   2 tons

3. Jan needs to sell more cookies to go on the trip. How many more cookies does she need to sell?

   5 pounds   5 ounces   5 tons

4. The pumpkin we grew is huge. How much does it weigh?

   37 pounds   37 ounces   37 tons

Ounces, Pounds and Tons

One - half pound (lb.) = 8 ounces (oz.)
1 pound (lb.) = 16 ounces (oz.)
One - half ton (T.) = 1,000 pounds (lb.)
1 ton (T.) = 2,000 pounds (lb.)

Complete the problems below.

1. 48 oz. = ___3___ lb.

2. 32 lb. = _____ oz.

3. 4,000 lb. = _____ T.

4. 80 oz. = _____ lb.

5. 2 lb. = _____ oz.

6. 8 lb. = _____ oz.

7. 3T. = _____ lb.

8. 6 lb. = _____ oz.

9. 16 oz. = _____ lb.

10. 12,000 lb. = _____ T.

Lesson 3

Estimating Length

Circle the best unit of measurement to estimate each item's length.

1. Length of your foot. (Inches) Feet

2. Length of your house. Inches Feet

3. Length of your pen. Inches Feet

4. Height of your dad. Inches Feet

5. Length of your car. Inches Feet

6. Length of your hair. Inches Feet

Lesson 4

Inches, Feet and Yards

12 inches = 1 foot	3 feet = 1 yard
36 inches = 1 yard	

Compare inches to feet.

Use the symbols **<**, **>**, and **=** to answer the questions below

1. 10 feet **>** 100 inches
2. 20 inches ____ 3 feet
3. 12 inches ____ 1 foot
4. 6 feet ____ 50 inches
5. 40 inches ____ 3 feet
6. 5 feet ____ 70 inches
7. 4 feet ____ 48 inches
8. 72 inches ____ 6 feet

Compare inches, feet, and yards.

Use the symbols **<**, **>**, and **=** to answer the questions below

9. 9 feet ____ 32 yards
10. 46 inches ____ 2 yards
11. 40 feet ____ 3 yards
12. 4 yards ____ 15 feet
13. 4 feet ____ 100 inches
14. 1 foot ____ 2 yards
15. 24 inches ____ 1 foot
16. 6 yards ____ 24 feet

Lesson 5

Ruler Measurement - Inches

Measure each object to the nearest $\frac{1}{2}$ or $\frac{1}{4}$ inch using the rulers below.

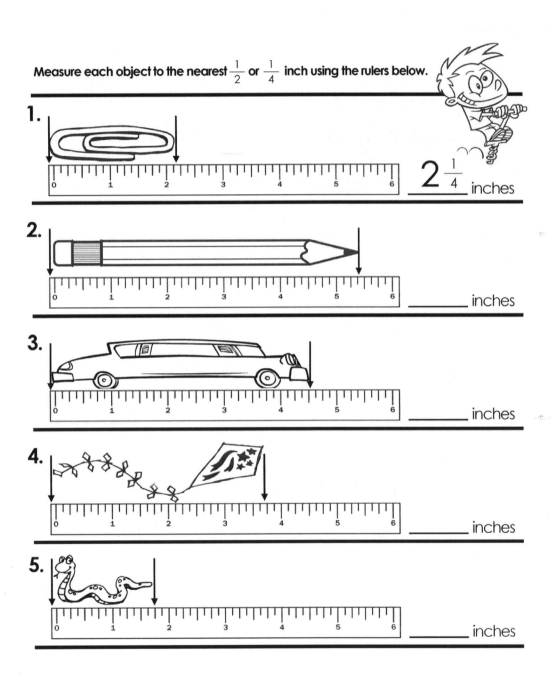

1. $2\frac{1}{4}$ inches

2. _____ inches

3. _____ inches

4. _____ inches

5. _____ inches

Ruler Measurement - Centimeters

Measure each object to the nearest centimeter.

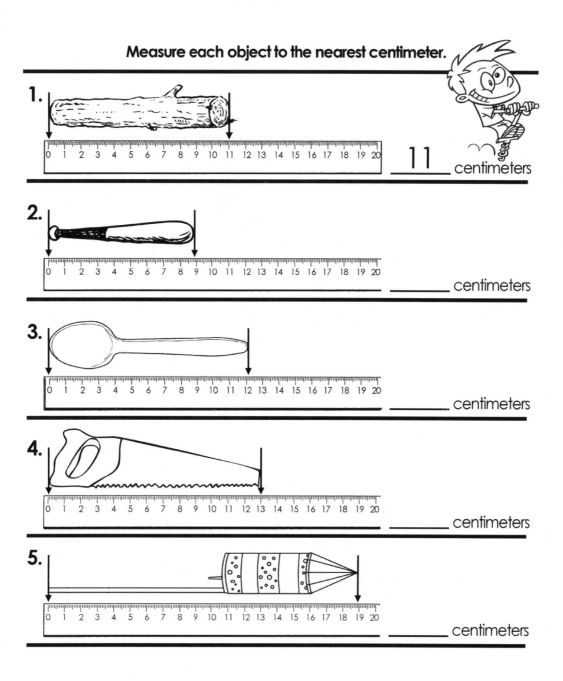

1. _11_ centimeters

2. _____ centimeters

3. _____ centimeters

4. _____ centimeters

5. _____ centimeters

Lesson 6

Liquid Measurement 1

| 2 Cups = 1 Pint | 2 Pints = 1 Quart | 4 Quarts = 1 Gallon |

1 Cup   1 Pint   1 Quart   1 Gallon

Circle the number of objects to match the amount in the box.

1.

2.

3.

4.

5.

Liquid Measurement 2

1 cup (c.) = 8 ounces (oz.)   1 gallon (gal.) = 4 quarts (qt.)
1 pint (pt.) = 2 cups (c.)   1 gallon (gal.) = 8 pints (pt.)
1 quart (qt.) = 2 pints (pt.)   1 gallon (gal.) = 16 cups (c.)
1 quart (qt.) = 4 cups (c.)

Complete the problems below.

1. 14 pt. = __7__ qt.   2. 3 c. = _____ oz.   3. 2 pt. = _____ c.

4. 16 oz. = _____ c.   5. 2 gal. = _____ c.   6. 2 gal. = _____ pt.

7. 32 c. = _____ gal.   8. 8 pt. = _____ qt.   9. 20 pt. = _____ c.

10. 13 gal. = _____ pt.   11. 10 gal. = _____ pt.   12. 24 oz. = _____ c.

13. 6 gal. = _____ qt.   14. 20 pt. = _____ c.   15. 48 c. = _____ gal.

16. 16 pt. = _____ qt.   17. 5 c. = _____ oz.   18. 6 pt. = _____ c.

19. 48 pt. = _____ gal.   20. 8 pt. = _____ c.   21. 16 pt. = _____ gal.

22. 112 oz. = _____ c.   23. 10 qt. = _____ c.   24. 3 gal. = _____ qt.

Liquid Measurement - Word Problems

Circle the correct answer for each question.

1. Mom is filling up the tub so I can take a bath. How much water does she need?

20 ounces   (20 gallons)

2. Danny's dog is thirsty; how much water should he put in its bowl?

3 pints   3 gallons   3 ounces

3. The car is low on gasoline. How much gas should we add?

12 cups   12 gallons   12 pints

4. How much paint should Rhea buy to paint her art project?

16 ounces   16 quarts   16 gallons

Lesson 1

Explaining Fractions

A **fraction** names a part of a whole. It can also be used to name a part of a group or set.

Fractions are made up of two parts. The **numerator** and the **denominator**.

$\dfrac{1}{4}$

⬤ ◯
◯ ◯

The numerator is the number of shaded objects.
The denominator is the total number of objects.

Write what fraction of each set is shaded in.

1. $= \dfrac{1}{3}$

2. $=$ ☐

3. $=$ ☐

4. $=$ ☐

5. $=$ ☐

6. $=$ ☐

7. $=$ ☐

8. $=$ ☐

Lesson 2

Comparing Fractions 1

- These fractions have the same denominators.

- We determine which fraction is larger by looking at the numerator.

- 6 is greater than 5. (6 > 5)

Numerator $\longrightarrow$ $\dfrac{6}{12}$ $\boxed{>}$ $\dfrac{5}{12}$
Denominator $\longrightarrow$

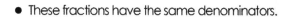

Compare the fractions. Write >, <, or =.

1. $\dfrac{2}{8}$ $\boxed{<}$ $\dfrac{4}{8}$

2. $\dfrac{1}{5}$ $\square$ $\dfrac{4}{5}$

3. $\dfrac{8}{10}$ $\square$ $\dfrac{6}{10}$

4. $\dfrac{2}{3}$ $\square$ $\dfrac{4}{3}$

5. $\dfrac{6}{7}$ $\square$ $\dfrac{2}{7}$

6. $\dfrac{10}{15}$ $\square$ $\dfrac{2}{15}$

7. $\dfrac{2}{6}$ $\square$ $\dfrac{4}{6}$

8. $\dfrac{1}{2}$ $\square$ $\dfrac{2}{2}$

9. $\dfrac{5}{10}$ $\square$ $\dfrac{3}{10}$

10. $\dfrac{3}{8}$ $\square$ $\dfrac{4}{8}$

11. $\dfrac{1}{11}$ $\square$ $\dfrac{9}{11}$

12. $\dfrac{3}{5}$ $\square$ $\dfrac{1}{5}$

13. $\dfrac{1}{3}$ $\square$ $\dfrac{4}{3}$

14. $\dfrac{1}{4}$ $\square$ $\dfrac{3}{4}$

15. $\dfrac{7}{9}$ $\square$ $\dfrac{5}{9}$

Comparing Fractions 2

Compare the fractions. Write >, <, or =.

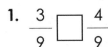

1. $\dfrac{3}{9}$ ☐ $\dfrac{4}{9}$

2. $\dfrac{5}{8}$ ☐ $\dfrac{7}{8}$

3. $\dfrac{3}{4}$ ☐ $\dfrac{1}{4}$

4. $\dfrac{1}{2}$ ☐ $\dfrac{2}{2}$

5. $\dfrac{7}{9}$ ☐ $\dfrac{5}{9}$

6. $\dfrac{6}{40}$ ☐ $\dfrac{16}{40}$

7. $\dfrac{10}{13}$ ☐ $\dfrac{12}{13}$

8. $\dfrac{6}{7}$ ☐ $\dfrac{5}{7}$

9. $\dfrac{9}{16}$ ☐ $\dfrac{2}{16}$

10. $\dfrac{10}{11}$ ☐ $\dfrac{2}{11}$

11. $\dfrac{2}{3}$ ☐ $\dfrac{2}{3}$

12. $\dfrac{25}{52}$ ☐ $\dfrac{4}{52}$

13. $\dfrac{60}{78}$ ☐ $\dfrac{9}{78}$

14. $\dfrac{1}{10}$ ☐ $\dfrac{2}{10}$

15. $\dfrac{2}{3}$ ☐ $\dfrac{4}{3}$

16. $\dfrac{1}{12}$ ☐ $\dfrac{2}{12}$

17. $\dfrac{1}{9}$ ☐ $\dfrac{2}{9}$

18. $\dfrac{23}{29}$ ☐ $\dfrac{4}{29}$

19. $\dfrac{4}{7}$ ☐ $\dfrac{6}{7}$

20. $\dfrac{111}{12}$ ☐ $\dfrac{12}{12}$

Lesson 3

Ordering Fractions

Write these fractions in order from least to greatest.

1. $1\frac{6}{10}, 2\frac{3}{10}, 1\frac{1}{10}, 2\frac{1}{10}$ $1\frac{1}{10}, 1\frac{6}{10}, 2\frac{1}{10}, 2\frac{3}{10}$

2. $4\frac{4}{8}, 9\frac{6}{8}, 6\frac{2}{8}, 9\frac{3}{8}$

3. $6\frac{1}{4}, 7\frac{1}{4}, 6\frac{2}{4}, 7\frac{3}{4}$

4. $8\frac{1}{9}, 9\frac{1}{9}, 8\frac{2}{9}, 8\frac{3}{9}$

5. $3\frac{8}{12}, 3\frac{1}{12}, 1\frac{1}{12}, 2\frac{3}{12}$

6. $5\frac{3}{54}, 5\frac{2}{54}, 5\frac{1}{54}, 5\frac{7}{54}$

Lesson 4

Adding Fractions with Common Denominators 1

To add fractions with common denominators, just add the numerators. The denominators will remain the same.

| Numerators $\longrightarrow$ | $\dfrac{2}{9} + \dfrac{3}{9} = \dfrac{2+3}{9} = \dfrac{5}{9}$ |
| Common Denominators $\longrightarrow$ | |

Add the fractions below.

1. $\dfrac{1}{5} + \dfrac{3}{5} = \dfrac{4}{5}$

2. $\dfrac{5}{10} + \dfrac{3}{10} = $ ___

3. $\dfrac{3}{6} + \dfrac{2}{6} = $ ___

4. $\dfrac{7}{12} + \dfrac{3}{12} = $ ___

5. $\dfrac{4}{9} + \dfrac{4}{9} = $ ___

6. $\dfrac{6}{14} + \dfrac{2}{14} = $ ___

7. $\dfrac{3}{7} + \dfrac{2}{7} = $ ___

8. $\dfrac{1}{4} + \dfrac{2}{4} = $ ___

9. $\dfrac{2}{6} + \dfrac{3}{6} = $ ___

10. $\dfrac{4}{8} + \dfrac{3}{8} = $ ___

11. $\dfrac{6}{11} + \dfrac{3}{11} = $ ___

12. $\dfrac{7}{15} + \dfrac{5}{15} = $ ___

13. $\dfrac{3}{14} + \dfrac{9}{14} = $ ___

14. $\dfrac{1}{3} + \dfrac{1}{3} = $ ___

15. $\dfrac{2}{8} + \dfrac{4}{8} = $ ___

16. $\dfrac{3}{5} + \dfrac{1}{5} = $ ___

17. $\dfrac{9}{13} + \dfrac{2}{13} = $ ___

18. $\dfrac{1}{10} + \dfrac{6}{10} = $ ___

Adding Fractions with Common Denominators 2

To add fractions with common denominators, just add the numerators. The denominators will remain the same.

Numerators $\longrightarrow$ $\dfrac{2}{9} + \dfrac{3}{9} = \dfrac{2+3}{9} = \dfrac{5}{9}$
Common Denominators $\longrightarrow$

Add the fractions below.

1. $\dfrac{2}{5} + \dfrac{1}{5} + \dfrac{1}{5} =$ _____

2. $\dfrac{15}{59} + \dfrac{3}{59} + \dfrac{9}{59} =$ _____

3. $\dfrac{4}{7} + \dfrac{1}{7} + \dfrac{2}{7} =$ _____

4. $\dfrac{6}{13} + \dfrac{2}{13} + \dfrac{1}{13} =$ _____

5. $\dfrac{4}{15} + \dfrac{4}{15} + \dfrac{3}{15} =$ _____

6. $\dfrac{44}{209} + \dfrac{19}{209} + \dfrac{7}{209} =$ _____

7. $\dfrac{6}{22} + \dfrac{1}{22} + \dfrac{9}{22} =$ _____

8. $\dfrac{4}{33} + \dfrac{1}{33} + \dfrac{16}{33} =$ _____

9. $\dfrac{3}{45} + \dfrac{10}{45} + \dfrac{11}{45} =$ _____

10. $\dfrac{63}{138} + \dfrac{23}{138} + \dfrac{18}{138} =$ _____

11. $\dfrac{1}{6} + \dfrac{2}{6} + \dfrac{1}{6} =$ _____

12. $\dfrac{3}{10} + \dfrac{3}{10} + \dfrac{1}{10} =$ _____

Lesson 5

Subtracting Fractions with Common Denominators 1

To subtract fractions with common denominators, just subtract the numerators. The denominators will remain the same.

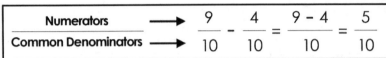

Numerators $\longrightarrow$ $\dfrac{9}{10} - \dfrac{4}{10} = \dfrac{9-4}{10} = \dfrac{5}{10}$ $\longleftarrow$ Common Denominators

---

Subtract the fractions below.

1. $\dfrac{7}{15} - \dfrac{3}{15} = \dfrac{4}{15}$

2. $\dfrac{7}{9} - \dfrac{2}{9} = $ ____

3. $\dfrac{12}{14} - \dfrac{7}{14} = $ ____

4. $\dfrac{8}{8} - \dfrac{6}{8} = $ ____

5. $\dfrac{28}{39} - \dfrac{19}{39} = $ ____

6. $\dfrac{24}{39} - \dfrac{11}{39} = $ ____

7. $\dfrac{9}{10} - \dfrac{2}{10} = $ ____

8. $\dfrac{13}{15} - \dfrac{9}{15} = $ ____

9. $\dfrac{13}{16} - \dfrac{3}{16} = $ ____

10. $\dfrac{6}{7} - \dfrac{4}{7} = $ ____

11. $\dfrac{10}{26} - \dfrac{8}{26} = $ ____

12. $\dfrac{60}{62} - \dfrac{41}{62} = $ ____

13. $\dfrac{19}{24} - \dfrac{10}{24} = $ ____

14. $\dfrac{46}{54} - \dfrac{17}{54} = $ ____

15. $\dfrac{98}{98} - \dfrac{15}{98} = $ ____

Subtracting Fractions with Common Denominators 2

To subtract fractions with common denominators, just subtract the numerators. The denominators will remain the same.

Numerators $\longrightarrow$	$\dfrac{9}{10} - \dfrac{4}{10} = \dfrac{9-4}{10} = \dfrac{5}{10}$
Common Denominators $\longrightarrow$	

Subtract the fractions below.

1. $\dfrac{23}{44} - \dfrac{9}{44} = $ _____

2. $\dfrac{6}{10} - \dfrac{4}{10} = $ _____

3. $\dfrac{30}{63} - \dfrac{19}{63} = $ _____

4. $\dfrac{45}{90} - \dfrac{42}{90} = $ _____

5. $\dfrac{12}{12} - \dfrac{6}{12} = $ _____

6. $\dfrac{28}{30} - \dfrac{8}{30} = $ _____

7. $\dfrac{4}{7} - \dfrac{1}{7} = $ _____

8. $\dfrac{15}{24} - \dfrac{6}{24} = $ _____

9. $\dfrac{45}{98} - \dfrac{31}{98} = $ _____

10. $\dfrac{5}{10} - \dfrac{2}{10} = $ _____

11. $\dfrac{5}{15} - \dfrac{3}{15} = $ _____

12. $\dfrac{8}{12} - \dfrac{3}{12} = $ _____

13. $\dfrac{20}{34} - \dfrac{19}{34} = $ _____

14. $\dfrac{6}{8} - \dfrac{3}{8} = $ _____

15. $\dfrac{14}{23} - \dfrac{7}{23} = $ _____

Lesson 6

Adding Mixed Numbers with Common Denominators

A **mixed number** is a number written as a whole number and a fraction.

When adding mixed numbers with common denominators,
add the whole numbers first, then add the numerators.
The denominators will remain the same.

$$1\frac{2}{4} + 5\frac{1}{4} = 6\frac{3}{4}$$ ← Numerator
← Denominator

Add the mixed numbers below.

1.
$$5\frac{3}{8}$$
$$+3\frac{2}{8}$$
$$8\frac{5}{8}$$

2.
$$2\frac{2}{5}$$
$$+1\frac{2}{5}$$

3.
$$9\frac{3}{10}$$
$$+3\frac{4}{10}$$

4.
$$2\frac{6}{15}$$
$$+2\frac{4}{15}$$

5.
$$4\frac{9}{21}$$
$$+5\frac{5}{21}$$

6.
$$7\frac{20}{42}$$
$$+6\frac{14}{42}$$

7.
$$13\frac{7}{9}$$
$$+3\frac{1}{9}$$

8.
$$12\frac{6}{29}$$
$$+11\frac{9}{29}$$

- 125 -

Lesson 7

Subtracting Mixed Numbers with Common Denominators

A **mixed number** is a number written as a whole number and a fraction.

When subtracting mixed numbers with common denominators, subtract the whole numbers first, then subtract the numerators. The denominators will remain the same.

$$9\frac{5}{6} - 4\frac{2}{6} = 5\frac{3}{6} \longleftarrow \text{Numerator}$$
$$\longleftarrow \text{Denominator}$$

Subtract the mixed numbers below.

1. $6\frac{3}{4}$
   $- 4\frac{1}{4}$
   $2\frac{2}{4}$

2. $8\frac{4}{6}$
   $- 3\frac{2}{6}$

3. $5\frac{8}{9}$
   $- 2\frac{7}{9}$

4. $9\frac{11}{13}$
   $- 8\frac{9}{13}$

5. $32\frac{15}{21}$
   $-18\frac{5}{21}$

6. $12\frac{7}{30}$
   $- 2\frac{2}{30}$

7. $17\frac{20}{26}$
   $-11\frac{12}{26}$

8. $25\frac{13}{17}$
   $-18\frac{8}{17}$

Lesson 8

Reducing Fractions 1

- Reducing (or simplifying) fractions means reducing a fraction to the lowest possible terms.
  - To do this, find a number that both the numerator and the denominator of the fraction are divisible by. Use that number as the numerator and denominator of a new fraction equal to one. Then divide the fractions.

Example 1:	Example 2:
$\dfrac{15}{20} \div \dfrac{5}{5} = \dfrac{3}{4}$	$\dfrac{3}{9} \div \dfrac{3}{3} = \dfrac{1}{3}$
$\dfrac{15}{20} = \left\lceil \dfrac{3}{4} \right\rceil$	$\dfrac{3}{9} = \left\lceil \dfrac{1}{3} \right\rceil$

Write the problems out and reduce the fractions below.

1. $\dfrac{5}{15} \div \dfrac{3}{3} = \dfrac{1}{3}$

2. $\dfrac{4}{12} \div \underline{\quad} = \underline{\quad}$

3. $\dfrac{6}{15} \div \underline{\quad} = \underline{\quad}$

4. $\dfrac{8}{10} \div \underline{\quad} = \underline{\quad}$

5. $\dfrac{10}{25} \div \underline{\quad} = \underline{\quad}$

6. $\dfrac{20}{25} \div \underline{\quad} = \underline{\quad}$

Reducing Fractions 2

- Reducing (or simplifying) fractions means reducing a fraction to the lowest possible terms.
  - To do this, find a number that both the numerator and the denominator of the fraction are divisible by. Use that number as the numerator and denominator of a new fraction equal to one. Then divide the fractions.

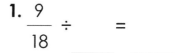

Write the problems out and reduce the fractions below.

1. $\dfrac{9}{18} \div$ _____ = _____

2. $\dfrac{6}{28} \div$ _____ = _____

3. $\dfrac{15}{18} \div$ _____ = _____

4. $\dfrac{12}{16} \div$ _____ = _____

5. $\dfrac{18}{36} \div$ _____ = _____

6. $\dfrac{24}{75} \div$ _____ = _____

7. $\dfrac{7}{49} \div$ _____ = _____

8. $\dfrac{27}{81} \div$ _____ = _____

Practice Test #1

Practice Questions

1. Donald has the amount of money shown below. How much money does he have?

Ⓐ $6.14

Ⓑ $6.19

Ⓒ $6.24

Ⓓ $6.29

2. Which fraction is represented by the diagram shown below?

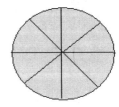 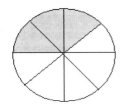

Ⓐ $1\frac{1}{8}$

Ⓑ $1\frac{1}{4}$

Ⓒ $1\frac{3}{8}$

Ⓓ $1\frac{1}{2}$

3. Which of the following models represents a fraction equivalent to $\frac{2}{5}$?

Ⓐ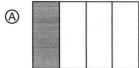

Ⓑ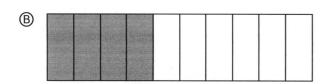

Ⓒ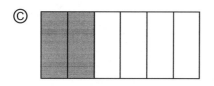

Ⓓ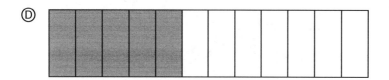

4. If Hannah drives 1104 miles a month and Carrie drives 1339 miles a month. How many miles do they drive each month combined?

_____

5. Jasper collects 1,082 cans of food. He gives a certain number of cans to the first local charity he finds. He now has 602 cans of food. How many cans of food did he give to the first local charity?

Ⓐ 430

Ⓑ 480

Ⓒ 682

Ⓓ 1,684

6. Which of the following models represents a fraction less than the fraction shown below?

Ⓐ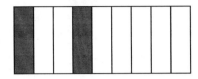

Ⓑ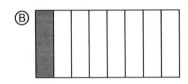

Ⓒ

Ⓓ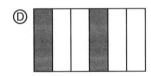

7. Amanda creates the base of a picture frame, using 4.55 inches of red fabric and 6.25 inches of blue fabric. How many inches of fabric are used to create the base of the frame?

Ⓐ 10.80 inches

Ⓑ 10.85 inches

Ⓒ 10.75 inches

Ⓓ 10.90 inches

8. Travis has a stick that is 5/16 of a meter long, and Steven has a stick that is 7/8 of a meter long. If they lay the sticks end to end how long would they be?

Ⓐ $\frac{12}{16}$ meter

Ⓑ $1\frac{3}{16}$

Ⓒ $1\frac{3}{8}$

Ⓓ $1\frac{1}{8}$

9. Which of the following number sentences is represented by the array shown below?

X X X X X
X X X X X
X X X X X
X X X X X

Ⓐ $4 + 6 = 10$

Ⓑ $4 \times 6 = 24$

Ⓒ $24 - 6 = 18$

Ⓓ $24 \div 3 = 8$

10. Which of the following number sentences is represented by the model shown below?

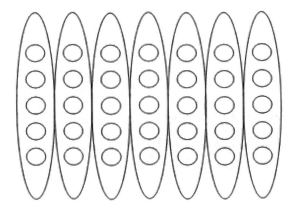

Ⓐ $7 \times 7 = 49$

Ⓑ $35 - 7 = 28$

Ⓒ $7 + 5 = 12$

Ⓓ $35 \div 7 = 5$

11. Hannah ran 12 laps every day for 8 days. How many laps did she run in all?

Ⓐ 108

Ⓑ 96

Ⓒ 84

Ⓓ 72

12. Kevin approved 13 trees out of every group of trees he surveyed. He surveyed 15 groups of trees. How many trees did he approve?

Ⓐ 155

Ⓑ 165

Ⓒ 195

Ⓓ 205

13. Monique has $690 to spend on a 3-day trip. She plans to spend an equal amount of money per day. How many dollars can she spend per day?

_____

14. Three friends sold cupcakes for a fundraiser. Eli sold 84 cupcakes, John sold 46 cupcakes, and Kim sold 72 cupcakes. Which of the following is the best estimate for the number of cupcakes the three friends sold in all?

Ⓐ 180

Ⓑ 200

Ⓒ 210

Ⓓ 190

15. Lynn has $316 to spend on groceries for the month. He plans to spend the same amount of money on groceries each week. Which of the following is the best estimate for the amount of money he can spend on groceries each week?

Ⓐ $65

Ⓑ $75

Ⓒ $90

Ⓓ $95

16. Carlisle charges $21.95 per hair cut and has completed 30 haircuts this week. Which of the following is the best approximation for the total charges for all haircuts?

Ⓐ $450

Ⓑ $600

Ⓒ $750

Ⓓ $800

- 134 -

17. Which of the following number sentences belongs in the fact family shown below?

$$7 \times 6 = 42$$
$$6 \times 7 = 42$$
$$42 \div 7 = 6$$

Ⓐ $7 + 6 = 13$

Ⓑ $42 \div 6 = 7$

Ⓒ $42 + 7 = 49$

Ⓓ $42 - 6 = 36$

18. Billy is going on vacation. He will travel a total of 1486 miles while he is gone. If Location A is 572 miles away from home and then Location B is 437 miles from location B. How long is the trip from Location B back to home?

_____

19. A door is $7\frac{1}{4}$ feet tall. How many inches is it?

_____

20. Mrs. Thompson writes the number sentences shown below:

$$100 \times 13 = 1300$$
$$100 \times 14 = 1400$$
$$100 \times 15 = 1500$$
$$100 \times 24 = ?$$

What is the product of the last number sentence?

Ⓐ 2200

Ⓑ 2300

Ⓒ 2400

Ⓓ 2500

21. The number of sit-ups Aisha has completed over a period of 3 days is shown in the table below.

Day	Number of Sit-ups
1	35
2	70
3	105

If this pattern continues, how many sit-ups will she have completed after 7 days?

_____

22. Which of the following correctly describes the relationship between the values of x and y, as shown in the table below?

x	y
1	4
2	8
3	12
4	16

Ⓐ The value of *x* is 6 less than the value of *y*

Ⓑ The value of *y* is 4 times the value of *x*

Ⓒ The value of *y* is 4 more than the value of *x*

Ⓓ The value of *x* is 1 less than the value of *y*

23. If the measure of angle *BAC* is 38° and the measure of angle *DAE* is 49°, then what is the measure of angle *CAD*?

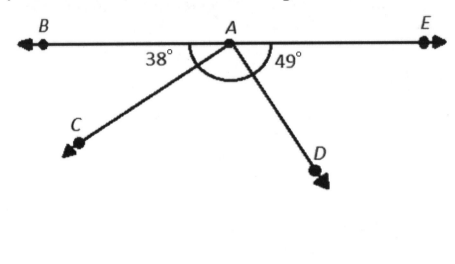

24. A farm has only cows and chickens. There are 5 chicken coops with 14 chickens each, and 6 barns with 16 cows each. How many total animals are on the farm?

Ⓐ 41

Ⓑ 330

Ⓒ 164

Ⓓ 166

25. Which shape has 5 sides?

Ⓐ hexagon

Ⓑ pentagon

Ⓒ octagon

Ⓓ heptagon

26. Given the numbers below, fill in the blank with the correct symbol (<, >, =) to make the statement true.

4.22 _____ 4.2

.09 _____ .9

2.72 _____ 2.702

27. Which of the following equation equals $4 \times \frac{4}{5}$?

Ⓐ $8 \times \frac{1}{5}$

Ⓑ $4 \times \frac{3}{5}$

Ⓒ $5 \times \frac{4}{5}$

Ⓓ $16 \times \frac{1}{5}$

28. The shape below represents a reflection about the axis. Which of the following statements is true?

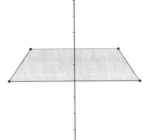

Ⓐ The shape has one line of symmetr

Ⓑ The shape has two lines of symmetry

Ⓒ The shape has four lines of symmetry

Ⓓ The shape does not have any lines of symmetry

29. What number is represented by Point A, shown on the number line below?

Ⓐ $7\frac{3}{8}$

Ⓑ $7\frac{1}{2}$

Ⓒ $7\frac{1}{4}$

Ⓓ $7\frac{3}{4}$

30. Which point, on the number line below, represents $14\frac{2}{10}$?

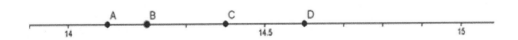

Ⓐ Point A

Ⓑ Point B

Ⓒ Point C

Ⓓ Point D

31. Which of the following are multiples of 7? Select all that apply.

    I.   **7**
    II.   **21**
    III.   **27**
    IV.   **39**
    V.   **42**
    VI.   **77**

32. Jason walks 2,847 feet to school. Kevin walks 3,128 feet to school. What is the difference in the distance that they walk to school?

_____

33. Ana draws a line with chalk that is $14\frac{5}{8}$ feet long. Then she erases $3\frac{3}{8}$ feet. How long is the line now?

_____

34. Which of the following are factors of 42? Select all that apply.

    I.   1 and 42
    II.   2 and 22
    III.   3 and 14
    IV.   4 and 11
    V.   5 and 8
    VI.   6 and 7

35. A box has a length of 7.5 inches, a width of 3.85 inches, and a height of 2.3 inches. Which of the following best represents the volume of the box?

Ⓐ 28 in³

Ⓑ 36 in³

Ⓒ 48 in³

Ⓓ 64 in³

36. Sally is making cupcakes. She needs $\frac{1}{4}$ cup of sugar for every 3 cupcakes. How many cups does she need for 24 cupcakes?

Ⓐ $1\frac{1}{2}$ cups

Ⓑ 8 cups

Ⓒ $\frac{3}{4}$ cup

Ⓓ 2 cups

37. Aubrey arrived at the party at the time shown on the clock below. It is now four-thirty. How much time has passed since she arrived at the party?

2:15

Ⓐ 1 hour, 45 minutes

Ⓑ 2 hours, 5 minutes

Ⓒ 2 hours, 15 minutes

Ⓓ 2 hours, 30 minutes

38. The bar graph below represents student preferences for different parks in Flagstaff, Arizona.

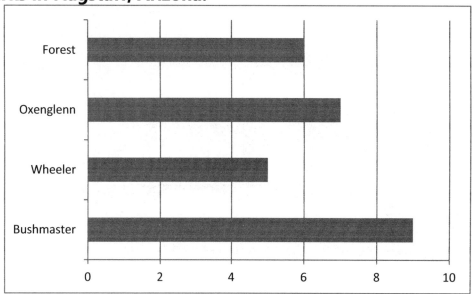

Which park is preferred by the most students?

Ⓐ Bushmaster

Ⓑ Wheeler

Ⓒ Oxenglenn

Ⓓ Forest

39. A cafeteria offers 3 meats, 3 vegetables, 2 breads, and 2 desserts. How many possible meal combinations are there?

40. The average number of miles per hour driven by a sample of drivers is shown below.

65, 70, 60, 55, 70, 65, 70, 60, 65, 70, 55, 65, 70, 55, 60

Based on the data, which average speed is driven by the most drivers?

Ⓐ 55

Ⓑ 60

Ⓒ 65

Ⓓ 70

Practice Test #2

Practice Questions

1. A room has 6 rows of 9 chairs. The room next to it has 32 chairs. Together how many chairs do they have?

Ⓐ 54

Ⓑ 56

Ⓒ 86

Ⓓ 84

2. Amanda buys a sandwich and pays the amount of money shown below. How much does she pay?

Ⓐ $3.56

Ⓑ $3.61

Ⓒ $3.50

Ⓓ $3.51

3. Which of the following sets represents a fraction equivalent to $\frac{8}{12}$?

Ⓐ

Ⓑ

Ⓒ

Ⓓ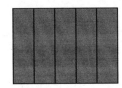

4. Which fraction is represented by the diagram shown below?

Ⓐ $1\frac{1}{2}$

Ⓑ $1\frac{2}{5}$

Ⓒ $1\frac{3}{5}$

Ⓓ $1\frac{3}{4}$

5. Which of the following models represents a fraction equal to the fraction shown below?

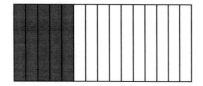

Ⓐ

Ⓑ

Ⓒ

Ⓓ

6. Which of the following fractions are equal to $\frac{2}{3}$? Select all that apply.

I. $\frac{1}{6}$

II. $\frac{6}{9}$

III. $\frac{4}{6}$

IV. $\frac{5}{8}$

V. $\frac{6}{10}$

7. Martin saved $156 in September, $173 in October, and $219 in November. How much money did he save during the three months?

   Ⓐ $538

   Ⓑ $569

   Ⓒ $548

   Ⓓ $576

8. Andrea pays $120 more in rent per month this year than she did last year. She pays $763 per month this year. How much did she pay per month last year?

   Ⓐ $663

   Ⓑ $643

   Ⓒ $863

   Ⓓ $883

9. Which sum is represented by the diagram shown below?

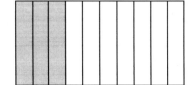 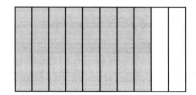

Ⓐ 1.08

Ⓑ 1.09

Ⓒ 1.10

Ⓓ 1.11

10. Which fact is represented by the array shown below?

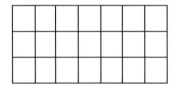

Ⓐ $3 + 7 = 10$

Ⓑ $21 - 7 = 14$

Ⓒ $3 \times 7 = 21$

Ⓓ $10 + 7 = 17$

11. Eli has 42 crayons and plans to give the same number of crayons to each of his 6 friends. Which number sentence can be used to find the number of crayons he will give to each friend?

Ⓐ $42 - 6 = 36$

Ⓑ $42 \div 6 = 7$

Ⓒ $42 \times 6 = 252$

Ⓓ $42 + 6 = 48$

12. Alex buys 3 gallons of milk each week. How many gallons of milk does he buy in 12 weeks?

Ⓐ 18

Ⓑ 24

Ⓒ 36

Ⓓ 48

13. A candle-making shop sold 18 candles on Friday, 37 candles on Saturday, and 23 candles on Sunday. Which of the following is the best estimate for the number of candles sold during the three days?

Ⓐ 60

Ⓑ 70

Ⓒ 80

Ⓓ 90

14. Isabelle must drive 1,482 miles. She plans to drive approximately the same number of miles per day over the period of 5 days. Which of the following is the best approximation for the number of miles she will drive per day?

Ⓐ 250

Ⓑ 300

Ⓒ 350

Ⓓ 400

15. A consultant earned $17,850 over the course of 6 months. Which of the following is the best approximation for the amount of money the consultant earned each month?

Ⓐ $2,500

Ⓑ $3,000

Ⓒ $3,500

Ⓓ $4,000

16. Mr. Jacobsen buys 32 boxes of oatmeal. Each box contains 20 packets of oatmeal. How many total packets of oatmeal did he buy?

_____

17. Mr. Johnson ordered 1 pizza for every 3 kids in his class. If he ordered 7 pizzas then how many kids does he have in his class?

_____

18. Part A: What fraction does the shaded area of the cirle below represent?

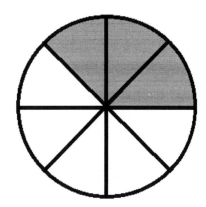

(A) $\frac{2}{3}$

(B) $\frac{3}{6}$

(C) $\frac{3}{8}$

(D) $\frac{1}{3}$

Part B: If 3 more slices of the circle are shaded in then what fraction would it be?

Ⓐ $\frac{5}{8}$

Ⓑ $\frac{5}{6}$

Ⓒ $\frac{2}{3}$

Ⓓ $\frac{3}{4}$

19. The number of miles Brad has driven over a period of 3 days is shown in the table below.

Day	Number of Miles
1	275
2	550
3	825

If this pattern continues, how many miles will he have driven after 8 days?

Ⓐ 2,000

Ⓑ 2,025

Ⓒ 2,075

Ⓓ 2,200

20. Andrew displays the following sets of data to his colleagues. Which of the following represents the relationship between the first and second columns of data?

4	16
7	19
12	24
14	26
19	31

Ⓐ The values in the second column are 12 more than the values in the first column.

Ⓑ The values in the first column are one-fourth of the values in the second column.

Ⓒ The values in the first column are 11 fewer than the values in the second column.

Ⓓ The values in the second column are 3 more than the values in the first column.

21. Jenny will be in a parade and will be throwing out candy. She has 20 pieces of candy, but she thinks that she will need 12 times that much since the parade is so long. How many pieces does she think she needs?

_____

22. Morris needs to define an obtuse angle. Which of the following correctly describes the requirements for such an angle?

Ⓐ An angle with a measure greater than 180 degrees

Ⓑ An angle with a measure greater than 120 degrees

Ⓒ An angle with a measure less than 90 degrees

Ⓓ An angle with a measure greater than 90 degrees

23. If John works 386 minutes a day, how many minutes does he work in a 5 day work week?

_____

24. Which of the following angles is acute?

Ⓐ

Ⓑ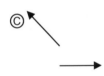

Ⓒ

Ⓓ

25. Sally eats $\frac{1}{4}$ of a pie, Jesse eats $\frac{1}{8}$ of the same pie, and Lisa eats $\frac{3}{8}$ of the pie. How much of the pie is left?

Ⓐ $\frac{1}{4}$

Ⓑ $\frac{3}{8}$

Ⓒ $\frac{1}{8}$

Ⓓ $\frac{1}{2}$

26. Part A: Which of the following figures does not have any parallel sides?

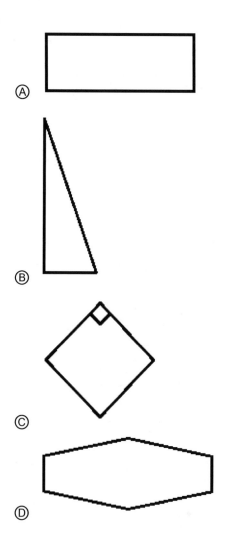

Ⓐ

Ⓑ

Ⓒ

Ⓓ

Part B: Which one does not have any perpendicular sides?

Ⓐ Figure A

Ⓑ Figure B

Ⓒ Figure C

Ⓓ Figure D

27. What decimal is represented by Point P, shown on the number line below?

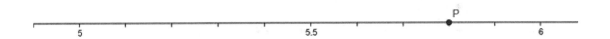

Ⓐ 5.6

Ⓑ 5.7

Ⓒ 5.8

Ⓓ 5.9

28. What Point represents $3\frac{3}{4}$, on the number line below?

Ⓐ Point A

Ⓑ Point B

Ⓒ Point C

Ⓓ Point D

29. A school has 14 classrooms. Each classroom has 22 students in it. How many total students are in the school?

Ⓐ 36

Ⓑ 288

Ⓒ 304

Ⓓ 308

30. Part A: A teacher took a survey of 4th, 5th, and 6th grade students about their favorite animals. Based on the results below how many total students were surveyed?

	Cat	Dog	Fish	Bird
4th Grade	8	10	5	4
5th Grade	10	12	4	4
6th Grade	7	13	2	3

Part B: What fraction of 5th grade students chose cats as their favorite animal?

Ⓐ $\frac{2}{3}$

Ⓑ $\frac{1}{3}$

Ⓒ $\frac{12}{30}$

Ⓓ $\frac{10}{28}$

31. Given the number 2,573. The number 5 is in what place?

Ⓐ ones

Ⓑ tens

Ⓒ hundreds

Ⓓ thousands

32. In the rectangle below each small square is one square unit. How many square units make up the area of the entire rectangle?

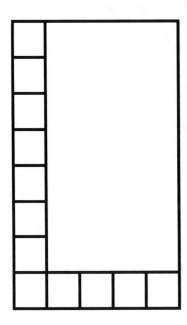

Ⓐ 28

Ⓑ 40

Ⓒ 12

Ⓓ 35

33. Hannah weighs approximately 27 pounds. What is her approximate weight, in ounces?

Ⓐ 432 ounces

Ⓑ 378 ounces

Ⓒ 324 ounces

Ⓓ 438 ounces

34. Jamal drinks 2 quarts of water per day. How many cups of water does he drink?

35. If Kara has 24 hair pins and she buys 6 more packages that each contain 12 hair pins. How many hair pins does she have now?

_____

36. Jim drives 1920 miles. He used 6 tanks of gas to drive that far. How many miles can he go on one tank of gas?

_____

37. Andy surveys his classmates to determine their favorite season of the year. The results are shown in the table below.

Season	Number of Students
Fall	7
Winter	3
Spring	12
Summer	18

Which circle graph correctly represents the results?

Ⓐ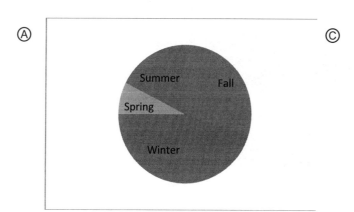

Ⓒ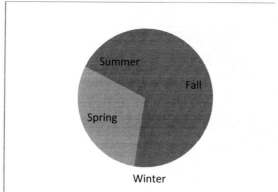

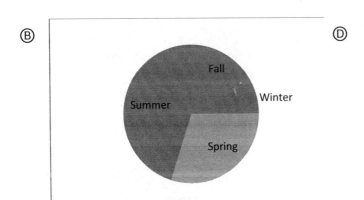

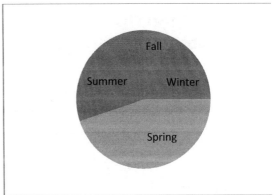

38. The bar graph below represents teacher preferences for different vacation states.

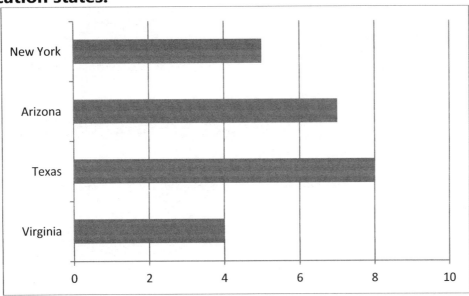

Which state was preferred by the fewest number of teachers?

Ⓐ Virginia

Ⓑ Arizona

Ⓒ Texas

Ⓓ New York

39. Alana can choose from 2 shirts, 2 pairs of jeans, 3 pairs of socks, and 2 pairs of shoes. How many possible outfit combinations can she make?

---

40. The scores on Mrs. Rodriguez's math test are shown below.

95, 78, 92, 99, 74, 83, 89, 92, 79, 85, 87, 90, 88, 92, 79

Which test score was received by the most students?

Ⓐ 78

Ⓑ 90

Ⓒ 92

Ⓓ 79

Thank You

We at Mometrix would like to extend our heartfelt thanks to you, our friend and patron, for allowing us to play a part in your journey. It is a privilege to serve people from all walks of life who are unified in their commitment to building the best future they can for themselves.

The preparation you devote to these important testing milestones may be the most valuable educational opportunity you have for making a real difference in your life. We encourage you to put your heart into it—that feeling of succeeding, overcoming, and yes, conquering will be well worth the hours you've invested.

We want to hear your story, your struggles and your successes, and if you see any opportunities for us to improve our materials so we can help others even more effectively in the future, please share that with us as well. **The team at Mometrix would be absolutely thrilled to hear from you!** So please, send us an email (support@mometrix.com) and let's stay in touch.

Additional Bonus Material

Due to our efforts to try to keep this book to a manageable length, we've created a link that will give you access to all of your additional bonus material.

Please visit http://www.mometrix.com/bonus948/fsag4mathwb to access the information.

TABLE OF CONTENTS

Workbook Answers

Chapter 1 - Place Value and Number Sense

Pg 6

1.

4	2	2	7	1	9
Hundred Thousands	Ten Thousands	Thousands	Hundreds	Tens	Ones

2.

9	8	2	1	2	4
Hundred Thousands	Ten Thousands	Thousands	Hundreds	Tens	Ones

3.

2	6	3	9	2	7
Hundred Thousands	Ten Thousands	Thousands	Hundreds	Tens	Ones

4.

6	2	7	1	4	1
Hundred Thousands	Ten Thousands	Thousands	Hundreds	Tens	Ones

5.

8	9	1	3	6	2
Hundred Thousands	Ten Thousands	Thousands	Hundreds	Tens	Ones

Pg 7

6	1	3	8	4	6	2
Millions	Hundred Thousands	Ten Thousands	Thousands	Hundreds	Tens	Ones

1.

3	1	9	4	6	7	5
Millions	Hundred Thousands	Ten Thousands	Thousands	Hundreds	Tens	Ones

2.

8	4	1	7	2	0	5
Millions	Hundred Thousands	Ten Thousands	Thousands	Hundreds	Tens	Ones

3.

2	7	6	5	4	4	7
Millions	Hundred Thousands	Ten Thousands	Thousands	Hundreds	Tens	Ones

4.

5	9	2	5	0	5	7
Millions	Hundred Thousands	Ten Thousands	Thousands	Hundreds	Tens	Ones

5.

Pg 8

1.   a. 3
       b. 4
       c. 1,000's
       d. 10's

2.   a. 3
       b. 2
       c. 10,000's
       d. 1's

3.   a. 7
       b. 4
       c. 10's
       d. 10,000's

4. a. 9
    b. 1
    c. 1's
    d. 1,000's

5. a. 9
    b. 5
    c. 1,000's
    d. 10,000's

Pg 9		Pg 10		Pg 11	
No.	Answer	No.	Answer	No.	Answer
1	900	1	3,000	1	80 + 2
2	200	2	9,000	2	20 + 9
3	600	3	1,000	3	50 + 6
4	600	4	8,000	4	70 + 4
5	800	5	3,000	5	30 + 5
6	300	6	4,000	6	90 + 9
7	200	7	6,000	7	200 + 50
8	600	8	8,000	8	600 + 20 + 9
9	400	9	6,000	9	100 + 50
10	100	10	2,000	10	800 + 90 + 2
11	9,000	11	40,000	11	900 + 5
12	4,000	12	20,000	12	400 + 20 + 7
13	3,000	13	90,000	13	20 + 9
14	6,000	14	60,000	14	70 + 1
15	7,000	15	70,000	15	80 + 6
16	2,000	16	80,000	16	50 + 4
17	9,000	17	30,000	17	10 + 6
18	6,000	18	40,000	18	30 + 8
19	2,000	19	20,000		
20	5,000	20	50,000		
21	50,000	21	300,000		
22	70,000	22	600,000		
23	10,000	23	200,000		
24	50,000	24	500,000		
25	90,000	25	200,000		
26	40,000	26	300,000		
27	20,000	27	900,000		
28	10,000	28	600,000		
		29	800,000		
		30	100,000		

Pg 12		Pg 13	
No.	Answer	No.	Answer
1	100 + 50 + 6	1	9,281 / 9,289 / 92,891 / 96,381
2	600 + 50 + 8	2	2,313 / 22,311 / 23,111 / 23,112
3	200 + 90 + 5	3	7,855 / 7,856 / 78,855 / 78,856
4	400 + 30 + 1	4	1,111 / 10,112 / 11,112 / 11,131
5	500 + 60 + 7	5	4,316 / 4,326 / 44,326 / 44,436
6	100 + 50 + 5	6	3,289 / 3,818 / 3,819 / 3,891
7	800 + 30 + 2	7	57,211 / 57,289 / 57,500 / 57,891
8	300 + 90 + 4	8	6,255 / 6,552 / 60,255 / 66,252
9	2,000 + 500 + 90 + 1	9	15,247 / 15,248 / 15,249 / 15,250
10	8,000 + 900 + 40 + 2	10	9,546 / 9,564 / 92,564 / 93,564
11	4,000 + 100 + 50 +4	11	8,219 / 84,218 / 84,219 / 84,921
12	6,000 + 300 + 80 + 7		
13	1,000 + 500 + 80 + 2		
14	3,000 + 500 + 70 + 8		
15	40,000 + 4,000 + 600 + 50 + 8		
16	70,000 + 3,000 + 400 + 30 + 5		
17	90,000 + 5,000 + 200 + 60 + 1		
18	30,000 + 7,000 + 800 + 70 + 2		

Pg 14	
No.	Answer
1	100,280 / 100,289 / 100,381 / 100,891
2	51,110 / 512,101 / 512,112 / 512,123
3	855,622 / 856,628 / 856,629 / 865,622
4	633,601 / 634,101 / 634,209 / 635,700
5	20,115 / 21,115 / 231,115 / 231,150
6	546,020 / 546,029 / 546,030 / 546,209
7	355,111 / 355,891 / 375,375 / 375,787
8	23,151 / 237,151 / 239,151 / 240,151
9	145,280 / 145,381 / 146,891 / 155,289
10	20,722 / 266,722 / 269,722 / 269,772
11	90,280 / 90,281 / 90,821 / 990,281
12	7,537 / 75,337 / 76,337 / 175,337

Pg 15		Pg 16	
No.	Answer	No.	Answer
1	10,495 | 11,005	1	980,311 | 980,411
2	98,311 | 98,411	2	622,001 | 620,001
3	61,001 | 63,001	3	282,929 | 283,029
4	22,929 | 23,029	4	694,647 | 694,667
5	81,657 | 83,657	5	113,729 | 114,729
6	2,495 | 2,505	6	349,001 | 351,001
7	12,303 | 13,303	7	524,303 | 525,303
8	41,370 | 43,370	8	805,370 | 825,370
9	72,126 | 72,133	9	156,119 | 456,119
10	34,776 | 35,776	10	619,776 | 629,776
11	69,061 | 89,061	11	120,383 | 125,383
		12	350,303 | 360,303

Chapter 2 – Addition

Pg 18		Pg 19		Pg 20	
No.	Answer	No.	Answer	No.	Answer
1	81	1	92	1	73
2	65	2	103	2	163
3	167	3	178	3	135
4	51	4	109	4	182
5	124	5	78	5	98
6	49	6	145	6	247
7	46	7	61	7	141
8	38	8	94	8	130
9	163	9	119	9	157
10	65	10	22	10	76
11	90	11	103	11	178
12	117	12	107	12	87
13	72	13	72	13	57
14	21	14	91	14	106
15	113	15	92	15	161
		16	155	16	146
		17	136	17	236
		18	125	18	138
		19	140	19	117
		20	162	20	286

Pg 21		Pg 22		Pg 23	
No.	Answer	No.	Answer	No.	Answer
1	114	1	64 apples	1	819
2	171	2	56 minutes	2	1,309
3	99	3	92 points	3	156
4	120	4	173 minutes	4	756
5	184			5	456
6	168			6	253
7	135			7	837
8	97			8	1,221
9	211			9	707
10	156			10	980
11	216				
12	146				
13	80				
14	197				
15	193				
16	181				
17	98				
18	134				
19	207				
20	49				

Pg 24		Pg 25		Pg 26	
No.	Answer	No.	Answer	No.	Answer
1	610	1	839	1	1,168
2	444	2	634	2	1,034
3	1,057	3	1,146	3	921
4	718	4	1,292	4	1,136
5	1,074	5	1,294	5	1,741
6	1,062	6	1,488	6	835
7	1,023	7	1,877	7	1,115
8	1,600	8	1,201	8	592
9	511	9	1,644	9	1,784
10	853	10	1,154	10	1,408
11	965	11	1,038	11	1,788
12	767	12	1,305	12	1,737
13	611	13	1,812	13	1,609
14	365	14	1,130	14	630
15	881	15	1,404	15	1,948
16	1,714	16	1,961	16	1,619
17	857	17	1,668	17	1,040
18	1,648	18	1,817	18	1,513
19	1,578	19	1,712	19	1,416
20	640	20	1,174	20	1,086

Pg 27		Pg 28		Pg 29		Pg 30	
No.	Answer	No.	Answer	No.	Answer	No.	Answer
1	12,301	1	6,515	1	51,648	1	104,349
2	10,761	2	16,834	2	100,997	2	49,815
3	17,388	3	12,670	3	100,116	3	70,804
4	5,201	4	13,229	4	40099	4	107,345
5	18,354	5	16,342	5	53,040	5	119,008
6	3,656	6	8,877	6	144,064	6	106,269
7	5,827	7	6300	7	101,610	7	133,061
8	8,464	8	11,866	8	62,008	8	40,277
9	11,656	9	13,940	9	73,875	9	72,695
10	3,875	10	16,715	10	71,664	10	34,262
11	8,347	11	15,009	11	47,770	11	72,436
12	7,886	12	6,461	12	37,380	12	99,053
13	14,419	13	15,177	13	105,374	13	137,107
14	5,328	14	15,408	14	181,336	14	82,013
15	10,061	15	13,512	15	63,471	15	69,809
16	9,571	16	24,745	16	115,422	16	143,052
17	5,567	17	10,693	17	116,456	17	81,492
18	7,669	18	14,319	18	58,785	18	88,374
19	6,145	19	14,792	19	88,523	19	106,406
20	4,859	20	14,112	20	123,973	20	111,110

Chapter 3 – Subtraction

Pg 32		Pg 33		Pg 34		Pg 35	
No.	Answer	No.	Answer	No.	Answer	No.	Answer
1	29	1	9	1	9	1	32
2	26	2	59	2	8	2	44
3	79	3	18	3	9	3	64
4	27	4	59	4	2	4	24
5	47	5	38	5	1		
6	36	6	23	6	3		
7	23	7	52	7	4		
8	9	8	9	8	9		
9	68	9	19	9	2		
10	24	10	3	10	7		
11	28	11	27	11	2		
12	28	12	14	12	1		
13	37	13	15	13	3		
14	19	14	21	14	3		
15	47	15	25	15	1		
		16	14	16	2		
		17	41	17	6		
		18	19	18	1		
		19	35	19	5		
		20	29	20	2		

Pg 36		Pg 37		Pg 38		Pg 39	
No.	Answer	No.	Answer	No.	Answer	No.	Answer
1	155	1	149	1	2	1	1,112
2	23	2	244	2	2	2	1,111
3	439	3	460	3	8	3	3,781
4	489	4	319	4	4	4	2,779
5	139	5	235	5	2	5	1,756
6	266	6	43	6	1	6	6,487
7	96	7	508	7	5	7	7,511
8	158	8	33	8	5	8	2,264
9	115	9	657	9	8	9	524
10	179	10	149	10	5	10	5,685
11	828	11	245	11	5	11	327
12	50	12	142	12	4	12	2,047
13	158	13	295	13	1	13	4,635
14	219	14	413	14	1	14	2,059
15	276	15	116	15	5	15	5,475
		16	159	16	9	16	2,889
		17	113	17	1	17	1,454
		18	283	18	3	18	916
		19	424	19	1	19	2,755
		20	151	20	1	20	2,747

Pg 40		Pg 41		Pg 42	
No.	Answer	No.	Answer	No.	Answer
1	1,616	1	13,148	1	1,697
2	1,158	2	15,814	2	40,444
3	488	3	22,552	3	13,887
4	1,634	4	4,247	4	22,986
5	1,159	5	56,697	5	15,585
6	2,858	6	28,313	6	25,802
7	2,215	7	34,340	7	32,578
8	6,651	8	36,202	8	36,857
9	3,491	9	20,488	9	17,909
10	888	10	24,740	10	15,799
11	2,464	11	13,056	11	21,239
12	4,405	12	4,166	12	31,847
13	1,109	13	38,183	13	42,887
14	4,465	14	36,482	14	1,193
15	3,117	15	22,675	15	36,487
16	3,280	16	19,121	16	52,142
17	4,384	17	18,498	17	18,489
18	3,409	18	26,282	18	21,529
19	2,135	19	1,348	19	17,435
20	6,933	20	37,376	20	44,217

Chapter 4 - Decimals

Pg 44		Pg 45		Pg 46	
No.	Answer	No.	Answer	No.	Answer
1	3.59	1	15.95	1	$5.03
2	7.83	2	664.48	2	$11.63
3	16.11	3	27.49	3	$9.22
4	14.16	4	40.97	4	$6.40
5	10.43	5	1,374.41	5	$12.75
6	74.36	6	622.28	6	$22.27
		7	10.53	7	$22.53
		8	54.25	8	$19.64
		9	118	9	$11.93
				10	$12.47
				11	$15.96
				12	$14.76
				13	$22.28
				14	$20.55
				15	$35.21
				16	$20.28

Pg 47		Pg 48		Pg 49		Pg 50	
No.	Answer	No.	Answer	No.	Answer	No.	Answer
1	$13.45	1	$10.16	1	52.64	1	93
2	$10.48	2	$6.23	2	7.2	2	13
3	$10.46	3	$17.64	3	38.28	3	33
4	$6.90	4	$13.64	4	15	4	25
5	$139.25	5	$17.50			5	58
6	$82.89	6	$96.27			6	65
7	$42.52	7	$107.95			7	83
8	$122.37	8	$101.99			8	42
9	$161.05	9	$40.12			9	69
10	$93.44	10	$75.61			10	20
11	$92.59	11	$170.83			11	34
12	$110.41	12	$161.41			12	32
13	$163.19	13	$354.25			13	77
14	$630.62	14	$1,184.55			14	72
15	$172.16	15	$1,530.84			15	12
16	$639.56	16	$533.92			16	44
17	$1,145.28	17	$1,460.97			17	46
18	$1,404.49	18	$1,101.03			18	56
19	$1,420.69	19	$1,870.40			19	21
20	$1,330.29	20	$1,003.80			20	19

Pg 51		Pg 52		Pg 53		Pg 54	
No.	Answer	No.	Answer	No.	Answer	No.	Answer
1	893	1	2.16	1	4.02	1	$2.47
2	113	2	34.62	2	50.35	2	$3.14
3	133	3	4.65	3	14.81	3	$3.18
4	25	4	326.28	4	42.91	4	$1.86
5	57	5	854.43	5	1.73	5	$1.15
6	765	6	68.99	6	581.61	6	$1.85
7	22			7	8.43	7	$3.77
8	342			8	255.15	8	$2.30
9	318			9	801.15	9	$3.13
10	920					10	$3.29
11	94					11	$0.39
12	32					12	$3.05
13	57					13	$4.79
14	672					14	$22.28
15	813					15	$13.54
16	544					16	$10.98
17	35					17	$7.77
18	812					18	$14.85
19	122					19	$7.77
20	698					20	$9.01

Pg 55		Pg 56	
No.	Answer	No.	Answer
1	$7.84	1	$12.18
2	$20.53	2	$3.21
3	$14.50	3	$3.18
4	$13.06	4	$30.10
5	$30.41		
6	$5.02		
7	$12.22		
8	$15.38		
9	$8.38		
10	$18.68		
11	$27.95		
12	$77.98		
13	$31.36		
14	$132.06		
15	$164.32		
16	$930.40		
17	$53.56		
18	$148.72		
19	$390.26		
20	$33.04		

Chapter 5 – Multiplication

Pg 60		Pg 61		Pg 62		Pg 63	
No.	Answer	No.	Answer	No.	Answer	No.	Answer
1	48	1	260	1	440	1	820
2	93	2	710	2	1780	2	590
3	86	3	670	3	2600	3	360
4	77	4	220	4	1170	4	910
5	55	5	380	5	1440	5	270
6	88	6	840	6	980	6	600
7	99	7	190	7	180	7	950
8	18	8	180	8	2640	8	890
9	84	9	940	9	4600	9	430
10	66	10	290	10	4690	10	270
				11	670	11	560
				12	1260	12	390
				13	270	13	75
				14	6750	14	10
				15	1500	15	88
				16	1320	16	62
				17	820	17	59
				18	1650	18	1
				19	2250		
				20	5490		

Pg 64		Pg 65		Pg 66		Pg 67	
No.	**Answer**	**No.**	**Answer**	**No.**	**Answer**	**No.**	**Answer**
1	92	1	84	1	284	1	1,302
2	406	2	150	2	663	2	663
3	172	3	52	3	682	3	1,705
4	261	4	558	4	484	4	1,732
5	180	5	198	5	698	5	6,282
6	220	6	425	6	848	6	848
7	288	7	182	7	396	7	396
8	495	8	176	8	466	8	1,864
9	198	9	288	9	696	9	2,088
10	354	10	342	10	282	10	1,098
		11	144	11	636	11	4,823
		12	264	12	336	12	2,995
		13	410			13	7,888
		14	261			14	738
		15	264			15	3,908
		16	236			16	1,110
		17	234			17	2,740
		18	378			18	2,432
		19	475			19	8,640
		20	276			20	1,590

Pg 68		Pg 69	
No.	Answer	No.	Answer
1	735	1	3,283
2	156	2	360
3	1,188	3	1,764
4	3,240	4	783
5	950	5	1,716
6	4,620	6	5,040
7	2,553	7	2,244
8	667	8	957
9	4,424	9	4,851
10	5,544	10	4,130
		11	1,053
		12	408
		13	3,182
		14	913
		15	5,529
		16	4,950
		17	1,650
		18	2,924
		19	3,404
		20	494

Chapter 6 – Division

Pg 72		Pg 73		Pg 74		Pg 75	
No.	Answer	No.	Answer	No.	Answer	No.	Answer
1	3	1	2 r 2	1	4 r 1	1	36
2	8	2	5	2	2 r 3	2	54
3	6	3	4 r 1	3	16 r 1	3	60
4	4	4	4 r 7	4	5	4	100
5	9	5	10 r 2	5	5 r 2	5	6
6	7	6	9 r 4	6	4 r 8	6	49
7	3	7	12 r 1	7	6 r 4	7	10
8	8	8	14 r 1	8	4 r 4	8	45
9	3			9	6 r 4	9	64
10	3			10	38 r 1	10	288
11	9			11	12 r 3	11	63
12	10			12	30 r 1	12	33
13	4			13	8 r 2	13	54
14	5			14	12 r 2	14	24
15	1			15	6 r 1		
16	11						
17	7						
18	15						
19	3						
20	8						

Pg 76		Pg 77		Pg 78		Pg 79	
No.	Answer	No.	Answer	No.	Answer	No.	Answer
1	8	1	$33	1	28 r 1	1	16 r 2
2	11	2	7 kids	2	24	2	21 r 2
3	2	3	3 dolls	3	16 r 1	3	42 r 1
4	6	4	9 cars and trucks	4	28 r 1	4	24 r 3
5	5			5	18 r 1	5	18
6	12			6	13 r 2	6	12 r 5
7	4			7	14 r 3	7	16 r 1
8	9			8	14	8	29 r 1
9	4					9	25 r 1
10	6					10	23
11	6					11	14 r 5
12	9					12	14 r 2
13	8						
14	9						

Pg 80		Pg 81		Pg 82		Pg 83	
No.	Answer	No.	Answer	No.	Answer	No.	Answer
1	246 r 3	1	164 r 3	1	11	1	32
2	49 r 3	2	171 r 2	2	22	2	48
3	296	3	206 r 3	3	8	3	54
4	256 r 1	4	89 r 3	4	33	4	52
5	216 r 3	5	32 r 1	5	21	5	71
6	186 r 4	6	382	6	22	6	60
		7	51				
		8	461 r 1				
		9	144 r 1				
		10	106 r 2				
		11	46 r 4				
		12	81 r 1				
		13	133 r 6				
		14	299 r 2				
		15	130 r 1				

Pg 84	
No.	Answer
1	84
2	20
3	140

Chapter 7 - Geometry

Pg 87		Pg 89		Pg 90	
No.	Answer	No.	Answer	No.	Answer
1	7, heptagon	1	cube	1	isosceles
2	4, square	2	cylinder	2	right
3	8, octagon	3	sphere	3	isosceles
4	1, circle	4	prism	4	scalene
5	6, hexagon	5	pyramid	5	equilateral
6	4, trapezoid	6	cuboid	6	scalene
7	9, nonagon	7	cone	7	right
8	5, pentagon	8	cube	8	equilateral
9	4, rectangle	9	sphere		
10	10, decagon	10	prism		
11	6, hexagon	11	cuboid		
12	3, triangle	12	cone		
13	8, octagon	13	cylinder		
14	9, nonagon	14	pyramid		
15	4, square	15	cube		
16	6, hexagon	16	prism		

Pg 91		Pg 92	
No.	Answer	No.	Answer
1	vertex	1	perpendicular
2	ray	2	parallel
3	line segment	3	intersecting
4	point	4	parallel
5	ray	5	intersecting
6	line segment	6	perpendicular
7	vertex	7	intersecting
8	line	8	parallel
9	vertex	9	perpendicular
10	point	10	intersecting
11	line	11	parallel
12	line segment	12	perpendicular

Pg 93		Pg 94	
No.	Answer	No.	Answer
1	obtuse	1	36 sq. in
2	right	2	36 sq. ft
3	acute	3	441 sq. in
4	obtuse	4	100 sq. ft
5	right	5	144 sq. yd
6	obtuse	6	81 sq. in
7	right		
8	acute		
9	acute		
10	right		
11	obtuse		
12	acute		

Pg 95		Pg 96	
No.	Answer	No.	Answer
1	140yd	1	18yd
2	25ft	2	39in
3	245in	3	38ft
4	125ft	4	70yd
5	175in	5	290in
6	163yd	6	216ft
		7	60ft
		8	75in
		9	48yd

Pg 97		Pg 98		Pg 99	
No.	Answer	No.	Answer	No.	Answer
1	3 ft³	1	20	1	500 in³
2	4 ft³	2	30	2	128 ft³
3	6 ft³	3	24	3	160 in³
4	5 ft³	4	36	4	720 ft³
5	6 ft³	5	48	5	240 in³
6	8 ft³	6	96	6	400 ft³
7	8 ft³	7	24	7	360 in³
8	7 ft³	8	30	8	245 ft³
9	7 ft³	9	60	9	162 in³

Chapter 8 - Measurements

Pg 102		Pg 103		Pg 104	
No.	Answer	No.	Answer	No.	Answer
1	60 pounds	1	3 lb	1	inches
2	2 tons	2	512 oz	2	feet
3	5 pounds	3	2 T	3	inches
4	37 pounds	4	5 lb	4	feet
		5	32 oz	5	feet
		6	128 oz	6	inches
		7	6,000 lb		
		8	96 oz		
		9	1 lb		
		10	6 T		

Pg 105		Pg 106		Pg 107	
No.	Answer	No.	Answer	No.	Answer
1	>	1	2 1/4	1	110
2	<	2	5 1/2	2	84
3	=	3	4 1/2	3	117
4	>	4	3 3/4	4	123
5	>	5	1 3/4	5	183
6	<				
7	=				
8	=				
9	<				
10	<				
11	>				
12	<				
13	<				
14	<				
15	>				
16	<				

Pg 108

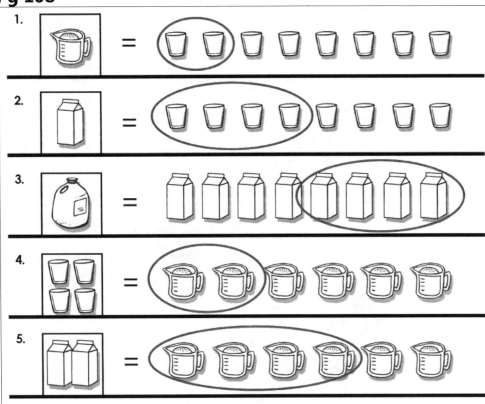

Pg 109			
No.	Answer	No.	Answer
1	7	13	24
2	24	14	40
3	4	15	3
4	2	16	8
5	32	17	40
6	16	18	12
7	2	19	6
8	4	20	4
9	10	21	2
10	104	22	14
11	80	23	40
12	3	24	12

Pg 110	
No.	**Answer**
1	20 gallons
2	3 pints
3	12 gallons
4	16 ounces

Chapter 8 - Fractions

Pg 112		Pg 113		Pg 114	
No.	**Answer**	**No.**	**Answer**	**No.**	**Answer**
1	1/3	1	<	1	<
2	2/3	2	<	2	<
3	1/4	3	>	3	>
4	2/4	4	<	4	<
5	3/8	5	>	5	>
6	4/8	6	>	6	<
7	3/16	7	<	7	<
8	9/16	8	<	8	>
		9	>	9	>
		10	<	10	>
		11	<	11	=
		12	>	12	>
		13	<	13	>
		14	<	14	<
		15	>	15	<
				16	<
				17	<
				18	>
				19	<
				20	>

Pg 115	
No.	**Answer**
1	$1\frac{1}{10}, 1\frac{6}{10}, 2\frac{1}{10}, 2\frac{3}{10}$
2	$4\frac{4}{8}, 6\frac{2}{8}, 9\frac{3}{8}, 9\frac{6}{8}$
3	$6\frac{1}{4}, 6\frac{2}{4}, 7\frac{1}{4}, 7\frac{3}{4}$
4	$8\frac{1}{9}, 8\frac{2}{9}, 8\frac{3}{9}, 9\frac{1}{9}$
5	$1\frac{1}{12}, 2\frac{3}{12}, 3\frac{1}{12}, 3\frac{8}{12}$
6	$5\frac{1}{54}, 5\frac{2}{54}, 5\frac{3}{54}, 5\frac{7}{54}$

- 33 -

Pg 116		Pg 117		Pg 118	
No.	Answer	No.	Answer	No.	Answer
1	$\frac{4}{5}$	1	$\frac{4}{5}$	1	$\frac{4}{15}$
2	$\frac{8}{10}$	2	$\frac{27}{59}$	2	$\frac{5}{9}$
3	$\frac{5}{6}$	3	$\frac{7}{7}$	3	$\frac{5}{14}$
4	$\frac{10}{12}$	4	$\frac{9}{13}$	4	$\frac{2}{8}$
5	$\frac{8}{9}$	5	$\frac{11}{15}$	5	$\frac{9}{39}$
6	$\frac{8}{14}$	6	$\frac{70}{209}$	6	$\frac{13}{39}$
7	$\frac{5}{7}$	7	$\frac{16}{22}$	7	$\frac{7}{10}$
8	$\frac{3}{4}$	8	$\frac{21}{33}$	8	$\frac{4}{15}$
9	$\frac{5}{6}$	9	$\frac{24}{45}$	9	$\frac{10}{16}$
10	$\frac{7}{8}$	10	$\frac{104}{138}$	10	$\frac{2}{7}$
11	$\frac{9}{11}$	11	$\frac{4}{6}$	11	$\frac{2}{26}$
12	$\frac{12}{15}$	12	$\frac{7}{10}$	12	$\frac{19}{62}$
13	$\frac{12}{14}$			13	$\frac{9}{24}$
14	$\frac{2}{3}$			14	$\frac{29}{54}$
15	$\frac{6}{8}$			15	$\frac{83}{98}$
16	$\frac{4}{5}$				
17	$\frac{11}{13}$				
18	$\frac{7}{10}$				

Pg 119		Pg 120		Pg 121	
No.	Answer	No.	Answer	No.	Answer
1	$\frac{14}{44}$	1	$8\frac{5}{8}$	1	$2\frac{2}{4}$
2	$\frac{2}{10}$	2	$3\frac{4}{5}$	2	$5\frac{2}{6}$
3	$\frac{11}{63}$	3	$12\frac{7}{10}$	3	$3\frac{1}{9}$
4	$\frac{3}{90}$	4	$4\frac{10}{15}$	4	$1\frac{2}{13}$
5	$\frac{6}{12}$	5	$9\frac{14}{21}$	5	$14\frac{10}{21}$
6	$\frac{20}{30}$	6	$13\frac{34}{42}$	6	$10\frac{5}{30}$
7	$\frac{3}{7}$	7	$16\frac{8}{9}$	7	$6\frac{8}{26}$
8	$\frac{9}{24}$	8	$23\frac{15}{29}$	8	$7\frac{5}{17}$
9	$\frac{14}{98}$				
10	$\frac{3}{10}$				
11	$\frac{2}{15}$				
12	$\frac{5}{12}$				
13	$\frac{1}{34}$				
14	$\frac{3}{8}$				
15	$\frac{7}{23}$				

Pg 122		Pg 123	
No.	Answer	No.	Answer
1	$\dfrac{3}{3}, \dfrac{1}{3}$	1	$\dfrac{9}{9}, \dfrac{1}{2}$
2	$\dfrac{4}{4}, \dfrac{1}{3}$	2	$\dfrac{2}{2}, \dfrac{3}{14}$
3	$\dfrac{3}{3}, \dfrac{2}{5}$	3	$\dfrac{3}{3}, \dfrac{5}{6}$
4	$\dfrac{2}{2}, \dfrac{4}{5}$	4	$\dfrac{4}{4}, \dfrac{3}{4}$
5	$\dfrac{5}{5}, \dfrac{2}{5}$	5	$\dfrac{18}{18}, \dfrac{1}{2}$
6	$\dfrac{5}{5}, \dfrac{4}{5}$	6	$\dfrac{3}{3}, \dfrac{8}{25}$
		7	$\dfrac{7}{7}, \dfrac{1}{7}$
		8	$\dfrac{27}{27}, \dfrac{1}{3}$

Practice Test Answers

Practice Test #1

Answers and Explanations

1. C: Donald has five dollar bills, which totals $5, and $1.24 in change; the sum of $5 and $1.24 is $6.24.

2. C: The diagram represents one whole, plus three-eighths of a second whole. Therefore, the diagram represents the fraction, $1\frac{3}{8}$.

3. B: The fraction, $\frac{2}{5}$, is equivalent to the fraction, $\frac{4}{10}$. The numerator and denominator of the given fraction are both multiplied by 2 to obtain the model for $\frac{4}{10}$; the fractions are proportional.

4.2443: To find their combined miles just add them together.

5. B: In order to find the number of cans of food he gave to the first charity, the number of cans of food he has left needs to be subtracted from the number of cans he collected; $1,082 - 602 = 480$.

6. B: The given model represents the fraction, $\frac{2}{9}$, which is approximately 0.22. The model for Choice B represents the fraction, $\frac{1}{8}$, which equals 0.125. This fraction is less than the given fraction. The fractions can also be compared by finding a least common denominator.

7. A: The sum of the two decimals is 10.80; the decimals are added just like whole numbers are, while aligning the decimal point.

8. B: If they lay the sticks end to end then you would just add the lengths together. First convert $\frac{7}{8}$ to $\frac{14}{16}$ then add that to $\frac{5}{16}$ to get $1\frac{3}{16}$.

- 37 -

9. B: The array represents the multiplication sentence, $4 \times 6 = 24$. Note. There are 4 rows and 6 x's in each row.

10. D: The model shows 35 counters, divided into 7 groups, with 5 counters in each group. Therefore, the model represents the number sentence, $35 \div 7 = 5$.

11. B: She runs 12×8 laps in all, or 96 laps.

12. C: Since he approved 13 trees out of every group of trees and surveyed 15 groups, he approved 13×15 trees, or 195 trees.

13. 230: In order to find the amount of money she can spend each day, 690 should be divided by 3; $690 \div 3 = 230$. Thus, she can spend 230 dollars per day.

14. B: The number of cupcakes sold can be rounded as follows: 80 cupcakes, 50 cupcakes, and 70 cupcakes, which sum to 200. Therefore, the best estimate for the number of cupcakes sold is 200 cupcakes.

15. B: The amount of money Lynn has to spend on groceries for the month can be rounded to \$300; $300 \div 4 = 75$. Thus, the best estimate for the amount of money he can spend per week is \$75.

16. B: The amount of money Carlisle charges per hair cut can be rounded to \$20; $20 \times 30 = 600$. Thus, his total charges are approximately \$600.

17. B: The missing number sentence in the fact family is the other division number sentence, which reads: $42 \div 6 = 7$.

18. 477: If he travels 572 miles and then 437 miles then he only has 477 miles left to go. 1486-572-437=477.

19. 87 in.: There are 12 inches in a foot. $12 \times 7 = 84$. Then divide 12 by 4 to get 3. 84+3=87.

20. C: As noted in the pattern, the product of 100 and 24 can be found by multiplying 24 by 1 and adding two zeros to the product. Thus, the product of 100 and 24 is 2400.

21. 245. Since she completes 35 each day, she has completed 35×7 situps after 7 days; $35 \times 7 = 245$.

22. B: The value of y is indeed 4 times the value of x. Note. 4 is 4 times the value of 1; 8 is 4 times the value of 2; 12 is 4 times the value of 3; and 16 is 4 times the value of 4.

23. 93°: Since the angle of a straight line is known to be 180°, then $38°$ *and* $49°$ can be subtracted from that to get 93°.

24. D: Multiply the 5 chicken coops times the 14 chickens to get 70. Then multiply the 6 barns times the 16 cows to get 96. Add those together to get 166.

25. B: A pentagon has 5 sides.

26. 4.22 > 4.2

.09 < .9

2.72 > 2.702

27. B: A rotation does not change the shape and size of a shape. Therefore, the rotated triangle is congruent to the original triangle.

28. A: The trapezoid is symmetric about the axis, thus showing at least one line of symmetry. The isosceles trapezoid does not have any more lines of symmetry. Therefore, it has one line of symmetry.

29. D: The number line is divided into fourths. Thus, between the whole numbers, 7 and 8, lie the fractions, $7\frac{1}{4}, 7\frac{2}{4}$, and $7\frac{3}{4}$. Point A represents the fraction, $7\frac{3}{4}$.

30. B: The number line is divided into tenths. Thus, between the whole numbers, 14 and 15, lie the fractions, $14\frac{1}{10}, 14\frac{2}{10} \ldots 14\frac{9}{10}$. The fraction, $14\frac{2}{10}$, lies two-tenths, or two intervals, to the right of 14.

31. I,II,V,VI: $7 \times 1 = 1, 7 \times 3 = 21, 7 \times 6 = 42, 7 \times 11 = 77$

32. 281: To find the difference just subtract. 3128-2847=281

33. $11\frac{1}{4}$: To find the length just subtract $3\frac{3}{8}$ from $14\frac{5}{8}$.

34. I, III, VI: $1 \times 42 = 42, 3 \times 14 = 42, 6 \times 7 = 42$

35. D: The measurements of the box can be rounded to 8 inches, 4 inches, and 2 inches. The volume of the box is equal to the product of the measurements of the length, width, and height of the box. Thus, the volume is approximately $8 \times 4 \times 2$, or 64 cubic inches.

36. D: If she needs to make 24 cupcakes and she knows the amount of sugar for 3 cupcakes then she just needs to multiply by 8. So $\frac{1}{4} \times 8 = \frac{8}{4} = 2$.

37. C: From 2:15 to 4:15, two hours have passed. From 4:15 to 4:30, 15 additional minutes have passed. Therefore, the elapsed time is 2 hours, 15 minutes.

38. A: There were 9 students who preferred Bushmaster Park; 9 students is more than any other number of students displayed on the bar graph.

39. 36. The possible meal combinations are equal to the product of the number of different types of each part of the meal. Thus, the possible meal combinations are equal to $3 \times 3 \times 2 \times 2$, or 36.

40. D: Five drivers drove at an average speed of 70 miles per hour, which is more than any other number of drivers, driving at a particular speed; three drivers drove at an average speed of 55 miles per hour, three drivers drove at an average speed of 60 miles per hour, and four drivers drove at an average speed of 65 miles per hour.

Practice Test #2

Answers and Explanations

1. C: The first room contains, $6 \times 9 = 54$, chairs. The second contains 32. $54 + 32 = 86$.

2. D: The amount of money she pays is equal to the sum of 3 dollar bills, or $3, and 51 cents, or $0.51. Thus, she paid $3.51 for the sandwich.

3. B: The fraction, $\frac{8}{12}$, is equivalent to the fraction, $\frac{2}{3}$. The numerator and denominator of the given fraction are both divided by 4 to obtain the model for $\frac{2}{3}$; the fractions are proportional.

4. B: The first diagram represents 1 whole, while the second diagram represents $\frac{2}{5}$. Thus the diagram represents $1\frac{2}{5}$, in its entirety.

5. B: The fraction, $\frac{5}{15}$, is equivalent to the fraction, $\frac{1}{3}$. The numerator and denominator of the given fraction are both divided by 5 to obtain the model for $\frac{1}{3}$; the fractions are proportional.

6. II, III: $\frac{4}{6}$ and $\frac{6}{9}$ can both be reduced to $\frac{2}{3}$. This means they are equivalent.

7. C: The sum of the dollar amounts is equal to $156 + $173 + $219, or $548.

8. B: Since Andrea paid $120 per month more last year, the amount she paid per month last year is equal to the difference of $763 and $120, or $643.

9. C: The diagram represents the sum of $\frac{3}{10}$ and $\frac{8}{10}$, or $\frac{11}{10}$, which is equivalent to $1\frac{1}{10}$, or 1.10. The decimals, 0.30 + 0.80, can also be added, which equal 1.10.

10. C: The array includes 3 rows and 7 columns. Thus, the array represents the number sentence, $3 \times 7 = 21$.

11. B: Since Eli will equally share his crayons, he will divide 42 crayons into 6 groups; $42 \div 6 = 7$.

12. C: Alex will be 3×12 gallons of milk in 12 weeks, or 36 gallons of milk.

13. C: The number of candles sold can be rounded as follows: 20 candles, 40 candles, and 20 candles. Thus, a good estimate of the number of candles sold is $20 + 40 + 20$ candles, or 80 candles.

14. B: The distance Isabelle drives can be rounded to 1,500 miles; 1,500 miles divided by 5 days is equal to 300 miles driven per day.

15. B: The consultant's earnings can be rounded to $18,000; $18,000 divided over 6 months is equal to $3,000 per month.

16. 640: Each box contains 20 packets, so that's the same as 32×20, which is 640.

17. 21: If 1 pizza feeds 3 people then you can multiply 7 times 3 to figure out that 7 pizzas feeds 21 people.

18. Part A: C: The circle is divided into eighths and then 3 of them are shaded.

Part B: D: If you shaded 3 more of the eighths that would make $\frac{6}{8}$ which reduces to $\frac{3}{4}$.

- 43 -

19. D: Brad drives 275 miles each day. Thus, the total number of miles driven, over a period of days, can be found by adding 275 miles to the number of total miles driven for each previous day. In other words, after 4 days, he drove 1,100 miles. After 5 days, he drove 1,375 miles. After 6 days, he drove 1,650 miles. After 7 days, he drove 1,925 miles. After 8 days, he drove 2,200 miles.

20. A: The values in the second column are indeed 12 more than the values in the first column. Note. 16 is 12 more than 4; 19 is 12 more than 7; 24 is 12 more than 12; 26 is 12 more than 14; and 31 is 12 more than 19.

21. C: The total amount of money donated is $300 more each additional year. Thus, the total amount donated, over a period of years, can be found by adding 300 dollars to the amount donated for each previous year. In other words, after 6 years, the total amount donated was $1,750. After 7 years, the total amount donated was $2,050. After 8 years, the total amount donated was $2,350. After 9 years, the total amount donated was $2,650. After 10 years, the total amount donated was $2,950.

22. D: An obtuse angle has a measure greater than 90 degrees. It may be greater than 120 degrees, but that is not a requirement.

23. 1930: To find the answer multiply 386 times 5.

24. A: An acute angle is less than 90°. Answer A id the only angle less than 90°.

25. A: First add all of the fractions together to find out how much of the pie was eaten. $\frac{1}{4} + \frac{1}{8} + \frac{3}{8} = \frac{6}{8} = \frac{3}{4}$, so that leaves $\frac{1}{4}$ of the pie that was not eaten.

26. Part A: B: A triangle does not have any parallel sides.

Part B: D: Perpendicular lines always form a 90° angle. None of the sides of a hexagon form a 90° angle.

27. C: The number line is divided into tenths. Thus, between the whole numbers, 5 and 6, lie the decimals, 5.1, 5.2, 5.3, 5.4, 5.5, 5.6, 5.7, 5.8, and 5.9. Point P represents the decimal, 5.8.

28. C: The number line is divided into fourths. Thus, between the whole numbers, 3 and 4, lie the fractions, $3\frac{1}{4}, 3\frac{2}{4}$, and $3\frac{3}{4}$. Point C represents the fraction, $3\frac{3}{4}$.

29. D: To find the answer just multiply 14 times 22.

30. Part A: 82: To find the answer add up all of the numbers in the table. This gives the total number of students surveyed.

Part B: B: There are 10 5th graders that chose cats as their favorite. There are 30 5th graders total. $\frac{10}{30} = \frac{3}{10}$.

31. C: The 2 is in the thousands place. The 5 is in the hundreds place. The 7 is in the tens place, and the 3 is in the ones place.

32. B: 8 units make up the length and 5 units make up the width. Area is length times width, so $8 \times 5 = 40$.

33. A: There are 16 ounces in one pound. Thus, her approximate weight, in ounces, is equal to the product of 27 and 16; $27 \times 16 = 432$. She weighs approximately 432 ounces.

34. 8. There are 2 cups in 1 pint and 2 pints in 1 quart. There are 4 pints in 2 quarts. Thus, there are 4×2, or 8 cups, in 2 quarts.

35. 96: If she buys 6 packages of 12 then she buys, $6 \times 12 = 72$. She already had 24, so 72+24=96.

36. 320: If he uses 6 tanks then 1920 can just be divided by 6 to get 320.

37. B: The circle graph can be created by determining the fraction of students, with preferences for each season. The total number of students surveyed is 40. Thus, 7 out of 40 students, or $\frac{7}{40}$ students, prefer Fall; 3 out of 40 students, or $\frac{3}{40}$ students, prefer Winter; 12 out of 40 students, or $\frac{12}{40}$ students, prefer Spring; and 18 out of 40 students, or $\frac{18}{40}$ students, prefer Summer. These fractions can be converted to the following percentages: approximately 18% prefer Fall, approximately 8% prefer Winter, 30% prefer Spring, and 45% prefer Summer. The circle graph, shown for Choice B, correctly represents these percentages.

38. A: There were 4 teachers who preferred Virginia; 4 teachers is less than any other number of teachers displayed on the bar graph.

39. 24. The possible outfit combinations are equal to the product of the number of different types of each clothing piece. Thus, the possible outfit combinations are equal to $2 \times 2 \times 3 \times 2$, or 24.

40. C: The score of 92 was received by 3 students, which is more than any other score received; 78 was received by 1 student; 90 was received by 1 student; and 79 was received by 2 students.

Additional Bonus Material

Due to our efforts to try to keep this book to a manageable length, we've created a link that will give you access to all of your additional bonus material.

Please visit http://www.mometrix.com/bonus948/fsag4mathwb to access the information.